CW00523651

The *Mindfulness* Diet

The *Mindfulness* Diet

Using Mindful Techniques to Heal
Your Relationship with Food

Madonna Gauding

Leaping Hare Press

First published in the UK in 2010 by

Leaping Hare Press

210 High Street, Lewes
East Sussex BN7 2NS, UK
www.leapingharepress.co.uk

Text copyright © Madonna Gauding 2010
Design and layout © Ivy Press Limited 2010

All rights reserved. No part of this book may be
reproduced or transmitted in any form or by any
means, electronic or mechanical, including
photocopying, recording or by any information
storage and retrieval system, without written
permission from the copyright holder.

British Library Cataloguing-in-Publication Data
A catalogue record for this book is available from
the British Library

ISBN: 978-1-907332-40-1

This book was conceived, designed and produced by

Leaping Hare Press

Creative Director PETER BRIDGEWATER
Publisher JASON HOOK
Art Director WAYNE BLADES
Senior Editor POLITA ANDERSON
Designer BERNARD HIGTON
Illustrator SARAH YOUNG

Printed in China
Colour Origination by Ivy Press Reprographics

10 9 8 7 6 5 4 3 2 1

CONTENTS

MINDFULNESS & THE FOOD YOU EAT

Mindfulness is an ancient Buddhist practice that helps you pay attention in the present moment to yourself and the world around you. The Mindfulness Diet applies mindfulness to the act of eating, thus offering an enlightening way for you to regain your health, normalise your weight, and bring joy and appreciation to your relationship with food. The Mindfulness Diet is not an ordinary diet with menus, prescriptions and restrictions. Rather, it works by helping you create a healthy relationship to your body, to the food you eat and to the act of eating itself.

WAKING UP TO EXCESS WEIGHT & OBESITY

◆

Mindfulness is a wonderful, transformative practice that helps us to pay close attention to what we are thinking, doing and feeling at all times. The practice of mindfulness can help us live life in the present moment, in a conscious, awakened state. When we are in an awakened state of mind, it is easier to confront difficulties and transform negative patterns.

THIS BOOK IS ABOUT bringing the practice of mindfulness to bear on something we have been collectively avoiding: the growing obesity epidemic around the world, and our personal struggle with eating and food. Diets function as a band-aid. They help us temporarily, but fail to offer what we really need: a way of relating to our body, our mind and the food we eat, that has the power to heal, once and for all, our overeating and obesity. It is time to take a new approach to reverse this alarming trend, which threatens to overwhelm the NHS and needlessly shorten our lives.

Bringing consciousness to the act of eating is the beginning of healing your relationship to food. The practice of mindfulness directly challenges the unconscious way in which many of us eat, which contributes to overeating and poor nutrition. Mindfulness will help you bring full awareness to your eating, an often distracted, automatic activity, so that you can begin to make better decisions about how to nourish your body.

> Mindfulness is the energy that helps us to be truly present.
> When you are truly present, you are more in control of
> situations, and you have more love, patience, understanding
> and compassion.
>
> THICH NHAT HANH, VIETNAMESE ZEN BUDDHIST MONK

Mindfulness will help you construct a healthy diet that is right for you, and restore your appreciation for the beauty of food and the sensuous pleasure of eating.

In the last decades, the food industry has introduced many unhealthy foods to the market, along with misleading and seductive advertising. The Mindfulness Diet will help you address any confusion you may feel around what to eat. The knowledge you will gain from this book combined with the practice of mindfulness will help you to distinguish healthy from unhealthy foods – and encourage you to choose succulent fresh, whole foods that deeply nourish the body and soul rather than the less nutritious alternatives.

There is much unexpressed emotional pain associated with ordinary diets. They are often based on the unspoken assumption that there is something wrong with you and your body as it is right now, and that you need to remake yourself into the likeness of an impossible ideal. The Mindfulness Diet assumes self-love and kindness towards yourself no matter what shape you are in. It rejects judgement, and supports

compassion and self-acceptance. Through an attitude of kindness and positive self-regard you can bring your body into a state of health and balance that is lasting and unique for you.

A WORLDWIDE OBESITY EPIDEMIC

◆

Before we explore the Mindfulness Diet, it is important to understand where we are today, and why we are having so much trouble with our food, our health and our weight. Over the past decade, doctors and pubic health officials have become increasingly alarmed at the growing rate of obesity amongst those living in industrialised parts of the world. Even though we tackle the problem by purchasing gym memberships, taking cardio-fitness classes and are spending vast sums on various diets and weight-loss programmes, we are losing the battle against obesity. In developing countries, obesity is on the rise and often coexists with poor nutrition. Collectively, we are heavier and less healthy than ever.

According to a 2006 World Health Organization [WHO] report:

• Globally, as of 2005, there were more than 1.6 billion overweight adults, at least 400 million of them obese. WHO projects that by 2015, approximately 2.3 billion adults will be overweight and 700 million will be obese.

• Obesity and being overweight are major risk factors for chronic diseases including type 2 diabetes, cardiovascular disease, hypertension and stroke, and certain cancers.

• The key causes of excess weight are increased consumption of energy-dense foods that are high in saturated fats and sugars, and reduced physical activity.

WHO recognises that obesity is not a simple issue. Rather, it is a complex condition, with serious social and psychological dimensions affecting all ages and socio-economic groups. Obesity rates have risen by about 300 per cent since 1980 in some parts of North America, the UK, Eastern Europe, the Middle East, the Pacific Islands, Australasia and China, and may be increasing faster in developing countries than in the developed world. Of especial concern is the increasing incidence of child obesity.

Why is this Happening?

Diets once high in complex carbohydrates (such as wholegrains, vegetables and fruits) have given way to urban diets of processed and ready-prepared foods. These have a higher proportion of saturated fats, salt and sugars, and are low in vitamins, minerals and other micronutrients. Western fast-food chains have spread worldwide, bringing with them foods that contribute to obesity. The high-calorie foods they offer are designed with addictive combinations of fat, salt and sugar.

EXERCISE 1

AM I OVERWEIGHT OR OBESE?

The body mass index [BMI] is a statistical measure of body weight and is dependent on both your weight and height. It is used to find out whether you are underweight, overweight or obese.

1 Your BMI is defined as your weight in kilograms divided by the square of your height in metres [kg/m^2]. Since height is commonly measured in centimetres, divide height in centimetres by 100 to obtain height in metres.

EXAMPLE: Weight = 68 kg, Height = 165 cm [1.65 m]
CALCULATION: $68 \div [1.65]^2 = 24.98$

2 If you are using the imperial system, the BMI formula is as follows: weight in pounds divided by height in inches squared, and multiplied by a conversion factor of 703 [weight (lb) / [height (in)^2] x 703].

EXAMPLE: Weight = 150 lb, Height = 5 ft 5 in [65 in]
CALCULATION: $[150 \div (65)^2] \times 703 = 24.96$

A BMI over 25 is defined as overweight, and a BMI of over 30 as obese. But even lower BMI levels can put you at risk of certain diseases, such as osteoporosis and damage to your heart.

At the same time, there is a trend towards decreased physical activity, which is partly due to the sedentary nature of many modern forms of work. Fewer of us walk to our destinations, and more of us drive or use public transport. Also, there are more labour-saving devices in our homes and we engage in more sedentary leisure pursuits such as watching TV, playing video games or surfing the Internet. Our bodies are built to walk, run and engage in other physical exertion, yet many of us remain motionless throughout much of our day. This fact alone is causing countless health problems for many individuals.

The Rising BMI

BMI is shifting upwards in many populations around the world. Adult mean BMI levels of 22–23 are found in Africa and Asia, while levels of 25–27 are prevalent across North America and Europe, and in some Latin American, North African and Pacific Island countries. BMI is higher among middle-aged and elderly people, who are at the greatest risk of health complications.

As you are reading this book, there is a chance that you are either overweight or obese, and have struggled in the past to lose weight. It would be good to take a moment right now to determine your BMI to know establish whether you are at risk (see box opposite). Your goal should be to use the Mindfulness Diet to get your BMI at least below 25, and ideally to around 18.5 to 20. While it can be alarming, it is important to examine the health consequences of not having a healthy BMI score.

Impact of Excess Body Fat on Your Health

Being overweight or obese has adverse effects on your blood pressure, cholesterol, triglycerides (fat levels in your blood) and insulin resistance. Health risks associated with obesity include respiratory difficulties, chronic musculoskeletal problems, skin problems and infertility. More serious, life-threatening problems fall into four main areas: cardiovascular disease (heart and blood vessels) and hypertension, insulin resistance and type 2 diabetes, hormonal related and large-bowel cancers, and gall bladder disease.

Your likelihood of developing type 2 diabetes and hypertension increases dramatically as your body fat increases. For example, 90 per cent of people with type 2 diabetes are obese or overweight. Once a disease of older adults, type 2 diabetes now affects obese children, even those who are prepubescent. Also, the incidence of diabetes is increasing in the developing world. If current trends continue, India and the Middle Eastern countries will have a serious problem by 2025, as will China, Latin America, the Caribbean and the rest of Asia.

Besides type 2 diabetes, an elevated BMI puts you at risk of developing cancer of the colon, breast, prostate, kidney and gall bladder. Being overweight or obese also contributes to osteoarthritis, which is a major cause of disability in older adults. Obesity, along with smoking, high blood pressure and high cholesterol, is one of the key risk factors for developing chronic disease. In a global analysis carried out for the World

Health Report 2002, a significant percentage of diabetes, heart disease and certain cancers were attributable to a BMI above 21. Clearly, excess body fat and weight is detrimental to your health.

THE PROBLEM WITH DIETS

◆

Although you may have sincerely tried to live a healthier life, you may be frustrated and demoralised by your efforts so far. Like many, you may have joined a gym but then felt guilty as you used it less and less. Your bookshelf may be filled with diet books, exercise regimes and cookbooks you have tried and discarded. You may have had some success – for a while – only to regain the weight you lost, and perhaps gain more as well.

IT HAPPENS SOMETHING LIKE THIS: one day you are doing fine, then you go to a party, overeat and the next day you slip back into old eating patterns. Overnight, you abandon your current diet. You soon find yourself eating, once again, when you are angry or frustrated, or because you need to reduce your stress, or to relieve your fear or loneliness. You may not even realise you are doing this, or if you do, you decide not to care. You just give up. The end result may be that you feel like a failure. You may suffer not only from the shame of being overweight, but from the added shame of thinking that you are weak and lacking in willpower.

But, as you will learn in this book, you are not weak, and there is no reason for shame. Part of the problem is that the cards are stacked against you – by the food industry, by the stressful pace of everyday life and by the standard approach of traditional diets. By the standard approach to dieting, I mean the tendency to treat food as an enemy, and your body as something to hate and punish. Diets that promise to turn you into a handsome, sexy man or an impossibly thin, attractive woman are an act of aggression against you, your body and your soul. Starting with an ideal is a recipe for self-hatred, and unfortunately self-hatred is often the motivation to lose weight. Perhaps you looked in the mirror one day as you were trying on clothes in a shop, and were filled with a feeling of disgust. Not liking what you saw, you left with a determination to change your body at all costs. It is no wonder that traditional approaches to weight loss often fail.

The Mindfulness Diet offers an alternative. It is built on a careful analysis of why it is so difficult to lose weight, and incorporates an extensive explanation of good nutrition. It offers a full understanding of what constitutes a healthy way of eating, combined with mindfulness practices to increase your awareness of your body, thoughts, mind and emotions. *The Mindfulness Diet* will help you to use mindfulness, along with an attitude of loving-kindness and compassion for yourself, to forge a new relationship with the food you eat. There really is a kinder, gentler, more enlightened way to have a healthy body and weight.

WHAT YOU WILL LEARN

◆

The Mindfulness Diet is divided into three parts: Part I, What is Mindfulness?, Part II, Your Relationship with Food, and Part III, Your Own Mindfulness Diet. Each part builds on the one before, so it is best to start at the beginning and work your way through each section at your own pace. There is no rush.

IN PART I OF THIS BOOK, you will learn about mindfulness. Although the ancient practice of mindfulness has its origins in the teachings of Shakyamuni Buddha, the founder of Buddhism, it is well suited to our contemporary life. If anything, the practice of mindfulness is needed more today than when the Buddha introduced it 2,500 years ago.

Everyday stress causes many of us to pull into our shell and live life on 'automatic'. We numb ourselves with unhealthy habits and various addictions, just to get through the day. If this sounds familiar to you, then rest assured that mindfulness practice can help you breathe, slow down and reconnect in the present moment – and with what is going on with yourself, and the world around you.

From a more alive and aware place, you can begin to make better decisions in all areas of your life, including in what you eat. Although mindfulness is a Buddhist practice, you don't need to be a Buddhist to do it. Mindfulness can simply be used as a tool for managing many aspects of life. It is even taught

in some hospital settings – for pain management, for stress reduction and for help in healing from serious diseases. As you will discover, mindfulness can be particularly effective in helping you heal your relationship with food.

In Part II of this book, you will look at *why* you eat, including the emotional reasons that may cause you to overeat or to eat unhealthy foods. You will also take a look at the food industry's advertising and marketing practices, which may be encouraging you to eat unhealthy foods as well as more than you actually need. You will then take a look at what you eat, and why the shift to more processed foods may be contributing to addictions and overeating. Finally, you will examine *how* you eat and how that affects your relationship with food. For example, do you eat and snack all through the day, do you eat on the run or do you eat alone in front of the TV? Taking a clear look at how you eat is an important piece of the puzzle in sorting out what is healthy and what is unhealthy in your current relationship to food.

Part III will introduce you to the Mindfulness Diet, which will help you find a new way to relate to yourself and to the food you eat. It begins with an introduction to mindfulness practice, incorporating a series of exercises in which you will learn to pay close attention to your body, your thoughts, your emotions and your senses. Then you will move on to the Mindfulness Diet basics: these are the tools you will need to heal imbalances, withdraw from food addictions and create

your own healthy way of eating. You will learn how to identify
the foods and situations that trigger overeating. You will also
learn what constitutes good nutrition, how to shop mindfully,
how to bring joy back into eating, how to have mindful
restaurant meals and how to eat mindfully at work. You will
discover how to find an exercise regime that is right for you.

RECORDING YOUR INSIGHTS

*It will help you to make progress with the Mindfulness Diet if you
keep a Mindfulness Diet Journal. This can either be written by hand,
or typed on your computer. Use whichever system works best for you.*

JOURNAL-KEEPING IS one of the best methods for uncovering
your deepest thoughts and feelings. You may find it one of
the most healing experiences you can have. It invites you to
dwell in an intimate, personal, sacred space where you can
begin to address the underlying emotional and spiritual issues
that are at the root of your problems. You will be asked to use
your journal for the following reasons:

• **To keep a record of what you eat.** Beginning now,
record what you eat for each snack or meal along with how
you feel physically, mentally and emotionally afterwards. In
this way, you will begin to see how certain foods may be

better for you than others. You can begin to identify which foods give you energy and which drain your energy, which make you feel bloated, which make you feel wired or anxious, and which ones help you to feel nourished and satisfied. Try to be as accurate as possible about the amounts that you are eating. Recording what you eat is a mindfulness practice that helps you to become conscious of what you are eating and how it is affecting your health and mood.

• **To record your insights when doing an exercise.** There are many exercises throughout the book that include writing as part of the task. Writing helps you to stay present and keep your focus, and brings to consciousness thoughts and feelings that you may not have been aware of.

• **To express your thoughts and feelings about your relationship with food.** Writing about your thoughts and feelings about food and eating – whatever spontaneously comes to mind – will help you in your journey towards a healthy relationship to food. Feel free to be creative. Write a poem, draw a picture, compose a song or simply jot down a new healthy recipe you come across. Write about your struggles and your discoveries. Feel free to express your emotions. If you are working on a computer, scan in any drawings and add them to your file.

• **To help maintain a kind and loving attitude towards yourself**. So much of the traditional diet mentality is punishing and shame-inducing, leading to the feeling that being overweight is an individual failure rather than a societal problem. Using your journal to counteract this misinformation will help you along your journey. Remind yourself on a daily basis that you are not alone in having difficulty with your relationship to food. Go back and read the introduction about the obesity epidemic affecting the world. Remember that this journey to rediscover healthy foods and healthy eating is also a process of ridding your body of toxins and food addictions. This transition requires patience and loving kindness towards yourself. There is no place in the Mindfulness Diet, or in your journal, for self-reprimands and harsh judgements.

• **To help you incorporate journal-keeping into your daily life.** Journal-keeping is an important aspect of the Mindfulness Diet. You can, of course, choose to stop when you have completed reading the book and working through the exercises. But hopefully, you will have begun a lifelong habit that will serve you well for the rest of your life. Your journal will keep you company as you maintain the new, healthy habits you will learn in this book.

PART ONE

WHAT IS MINDFULNESS?

Mindfulness is present, engaged awareness. It is a process of continual observation and attention as you experience the ongoing flow of your changing sensory awareness and perceptions.When you are mindful you are not passive: you bring intention to whatever you are doing. Mindfulness is paying attention, without judgement, to what is going on inside of you, emotionally and physically, and what is going on around you in your environment.

A BUDDHIST APPROACH
TO THE PROBLEM OF OVEREATING

◆

The Buddha advocated the search for the Middle Path — one that avoids rigid extremes, harsh all-or-nothing judgements, and conditioned 'black and white' thought. In other words, he taught moderation in all things. He aimed to teach his students what he discovered himself — his ability to focus his mind on the present, what is in the here and now, so as to fully embrace his existence. He taught them to accept 'what is' and to avoid the extremes of interpretation and judgement of others and self. The 'acceptance of what is', was the root of compassion. He wanted to wake up his students from their conditioned, unconscious, impulsive thinking and behaviour, to help them achieve the freedom of conscious choice.

IF THE BUDDHA were a psychologist today, he would surely help you to modify the unconscious negative patterns that cause you to overeat and compromise your health, and help you to ground your life in clear, awakened awareness and self-love. He would teach mindfulness to help you recover from food addictions and help you to restore a healthy, pleasurable 'Middle Way' relationship to food and eating. He would begin with helping you to examine how your mind usually works.

In your normal state of mind, your thoughts often jump from one to the other, each triggering another. You may drive to work using your usual route, say, and be so lost in these

thoughts that you fail to notice anything along the way. In a state of mindfulness, you can turn your attention to watching those thoughts as an impartial observer, or to noticing whether your body is feeling pain or cold or another sensation. You may become aware that the trees along your route are beginning to change or that the sky is threatening rain or that the lorry in front of you is driving a bit erratically, prompting more caution on your part.

Through deliberate focused awareness, you can take a break from being lost in thought and in the emotions triggered by them, and turn your awareness to the present. In the practice of mindfulness, there is nothing but the present. Life lived fully in the present is, by nature, rich, full and deep.

With practice, mindfulness cultivates the possibility of freeing yourself of reactive, habitual patterns of thinking, feeling and acting, including overindulging in food or eating foods that are unhealthy for you. Mindfulness promotes balance by helping you avoid extremes of thought and action. It gives you access to the infinite opportunities and choices inherent in the present moment, whereas mentally living in the past or the future limits your possibilities. Mindfulness promotes intelligence and wisdom because the mindful mind is necessarily alive and fully awake, and it promotes compassion through non-judgemental acceptance of what is.

AN ANCIENT PRACTICE FOR MODERN TIMES

◆

The historical Buddha, Buddha Shakyamuni, lived in India around 500 BCE. He began life as a prince, and lived a sheltered, idyllic life where only young, beautiful people surrounded him. One day, out of curiosity, he left the palace compound and was shocked at the sight of old people, sick people and all manner of human suffering around him. He was so moved that he left his privileged life and became a spiritual seeker. Out of compassion he wanted to discover how to remedy the pain he witnessed.

H E SET ABOUT WANDERING with like-minded people, trying various spiritual practices and engaging with the most respected teachers of the day. Ultimately, he became dissatisfied with the path he was on, and set out on his own to discover how to end suffering and understand the true meaning of life. After many years of trial and error, he eventually managed to achieve enlightenment. He did not plan to teach others how to do the same, but those close to him, seeing his transformation and his release from his own suffering, begged him to reveal his methods.

One of the most healing and effective practices the Buddha taught was the practice of mindfulness. He discovered that we create our world and our reality in the present moment, and therefore it is crucial to learn to pay attention to the present. He knew, by watching his own thoughts, that the human mind

is constantly swinging into the future or back to the past, spending very little time in the present. He was not saying, however, that we should avoid memory or imagination, and live in a strange eternal 'now'. But he did see that in order to get beyond our confusion and suffering, we need to train ourselves to see how we distort reality by continually bringing the past and the future into the present. To cut our confusion he advocated that we practise being fully mindful of what is happening right now.

Left to its own inclinations, our mind would much rather construct a story about the present moment rather than see and experience it fresh and clear-eyed. For example, we may construct a believable story about why we deserve a piece of chocolate cake every day instead of seeing it for what it is – a food laden with sugar, refined flour and fat that may be causing harm to our body. But that is not to say that mindfulness is a road to pain and deprivation. Rather, it is about cultivating the ability to make good, nurturing, healing choices for our selves as we move through life. For example, through the practice of mindfulness we can learn to transition from an out-of-control addiction to, say, ice cream, to the fully satisfying experience of eating fresh wholesome foods.

Through mindfulness, we can carefully and gently see what is unfolding in the immediate present moment, which is the only time we ever really have. This is the revolutionary path of healing that the Buddha taught.

LIVING ON AUTOMATIC

◆

You, like all of us, are a creature of habit – and habits and routines can be good things. Having routines makes your days easier. It means that you don't have to make a decision over every little thing you do. For example, you know when to set the alarm, and how long to allow for breakfast and for the drive to work. You probably have a routine when you get there – perhaps you get your coffee, chat with your work colleagues for a few minutes, check your email and then get on with the day's activities. Your day is all worked out for you.

HAVING ROUTINES can allow you to do what is necessary whilst thinking about something else – whether you are showering, eating breakfast or driving to work. So, your mind may wander to your next holiday as you work on a report due tomorrow, for example. It may seem normal and familiar to be distracted, and you even celebrate your ability to 'multitask'. You may eat lunch at a fast-food restaurant, and read the paper whilst you wolf down a burger, chips and a diet cola. Then you may race back to work after taking a mint to quiet your indigestion. On the drive home, you may be thinking about a conversation you need to have with your partner about finances. Perhaps this makes you tense.

The truth is the report you were working on today could have been better – if you were really paying attention. If you had mindfully assessed the health consequences of eating

the 'burger special' for lunch, you may have opted for a healthier, more satisfying choice. The sunset on the drive home may have relaxed you in preparation for a difficult conversation, if you could only have noticed it.

We are very good at living on 'automatic'. We go through the motions in the present but we are mostly living in the past or the future. In this way we can actually miss much of our life. It is like we are on a scenic bus tour but we keep our head in a book the whole way. We miss the beautiful sights, smells, tastes, sounds and textures that we could enjoy if we only turned our focused awareness to what is going on right now. To see our lover's face and look into his or her eyes can be a profound experience. But often we fail to open to those closest to us because we are too caught up in our own thoughts, our fears about the future or our past hurts.

When it comes to food, being present in the moment whilst preparing and eating meals can be a profoundly healing experience. To taste a succulent peach, or a piece of freshly baked wholegrain bread, to be really present with the act of eating can be transformative, as we will see.

We go through the motions in the present but we are mostly living in the past or the future.

EXERCISE 2

LEARNING TO PAY ATTENTION

Mindfulness is the art of paying attention. It is through focusing your attention on what you eat, why you eat and how you eat that you will begin to heal your relationship to food. One way to practise paying attention is to meditate on your breath. This very simple practice helps you learn to focus and calm your mind.

1 Wear comfortable, loose clothing, and sit on a straight-backed chair with your feet flat on the floor. Sit slightly forwards on the chair, with your spine straight and your shoulders relaxed, without using the chair back for support. Allow your hands to rest comfortably in your lap.

2 Your head should be level and your eyes open but softly focused on a spot on the floor about 1 m (3 ft) in front of you. Make sure you are comfortable and relaxed. Let go of any tension in your body, then rock gently from side to side until you find a natural point of balance.

3 Take a few deep breaths into your abdomen, allowing your breath to rise and fill your lungs. This type of breathing moves your diaphragm downwards, allowing your lungs to fill more easily. After a few exaggerated deep breaths continue to breathe normally into your abdomen.

4 Now simply focus on your breath itself. You can do this by focusing on the sensation of air moving over your upper lip, or you can focus on the sensation of your abdomen rising and falling, or you can simply count your breaths one to ten and then start over. Put all your attention on your breath and try to empty your mind of all thoughts. When a thought arises, simply bring your attention back to your breath as you gently and lovingly would bring a small child back to your side.

5 It will be difficult to empty your mind of thoughts. And you will have to bring your attention back to your breath hundreds of times. But after ten minutes or so, you will begin to feel the calming effects of being mindful of your breath, and you will have a taste of what being present in the moment feels like. You may, for example, feel more aware of your body. You may miss your normal constant stream of thoughts and their attending emotions. Then again, simply focusing on your breath may release feelings of sadness or anger that you have been suppressing. Or you may simply enjoy the peace and relaxation. There is no right or wrong way to do this meditation. Simply experience it.

6 Meditate for 15 minutes or more and when you are ready, end your meditation. Then, write in your journal about what you experienced physically, mentally and emotionally, and what you enjoyed or found uncomfortable about the process.

MAKING GOOD DECISIONS FOR YOURSELF

When you learn to pay attention to what is happening right now, you can make better decisions for yourself and for others in your care. You are much less likely to be held back by fear or other difficult emotions. For example, if a loved one clutches his chest and falls to the floor at dinner, it may trigger a memory of your father dying of a heart attack and leaving your mother alone and bereft. This memory may flood your mind, adding more fear to an already fearful situation. As a result, you lose precious moments before you call for an ambulance. You feel paralyzed, momentarily, with visions of spending your life alone without the person that you love.

MINDFULNESS IS not without emotion, but the ability to pay attention to what is going on right now without the overlay of past memories and future fears, may make you more effective in dealing with difficult instances, such as an accident or an emergency. Mindfulness in your every-day life helps you to make better choices for your health, including what you eat. With examination, you may discover that many of your food choices are based on habit and even addiction. For example, you may eat a high-fat, high-calorie, high-sugar breakfast every morning because you have grown used to it, so much so you begin to crave it. It seems it is impossible to start your day without a large dose of caffeine and a sugary pastry of some kind. Eventually you may start

> Unfortunately there are few daily activities that
> are so loaded with pain and distress, with guilt and
> shame, with unfulfilled longing and despair than
> the simple act of putting energy into our bodies.
> When we learn to eat mindfully, our eating can be
> transformed from a source of suffering to a source
> of renewal, self-understanding and delight.
>
> JAN CHOZEN BAYS, AMERICAN ZEN BUDDHIST
> TEACHER & PHYSICIAN

eating two pastries instead of one. You may have come to believe that the jolt of energy you get from a high-sugar spike and the rush of caffeine helps you to function better at work.

By practising mindfulness, you can begin to see clearly what you are doing to your health, and then make the transition, at your own pace, to foods that give you true nutrition and energy, and that better serve you mentally and physically throughout the day. You will learn to question your current belief that you need unhealthy foods to function, and instead, make a loving, healthy choice for yourself in the present.

Whether caring for those you love, or caring for yourself, mindfulness clears away the past memories and future fantasies that cloud your present experience and perception. In that clear, wise state, you can make the right choices for yourself and for others.

EXERCISE 3

A MINDFUL BREAKFAST

This exercise will introduce you to the practice of mindfulness as you prepare and eat your breakfast. Try this on a weekend when you can be free from worries about getting the children off to school or getting yourself to work. In this exercise you will try as best you can to avoid thinking and pay attention with intense focus to everything you are doing.

1 Take the food for your breakfast from the fridge or the cupboard, and place it on the kitchen work surface.

2 Prepare or cook your breakfast. Whilst you are doing this, focus on each movement you make – as you pick up a bowl or utensil or step to the sink or cooker. When your thoughts begin to wander, simply bring your focus back to your senses and what you are doing. Pay attention to sound, colour, smell, taste and the texture of everything around you. Notice the light in the kitchen and the temperature in the room. Be aware of how your body feels: is it tense or relaxed? Pay attention to how your food, the dishes or saucepans look, and how they sound when picked up and moved. Notice the beauty of the fresh bread, the eggs, the fruit or cereal. Move slowly and deliberately. There is no rush. If this makes you nervous at all, simply breathe into your abdomen with a few long slow breaths.

3 After you have prepared your breakfast, place it on the table in a way that is pleasing to you. Sit down and take a moment to express gratitude for the food you are about to eat.

4 Take a few moments to notice the colours, textures and aromas of the food in front of you. Next, slowly pick up your utensil, or your toast, and begin to eat slowly. When thoughts begin to take over your mind – and they will – simply bring your attention back to what you are doing. You will do this over and over again; learning to be fully present takes practise. Try to eat your whole breakfast slowly, and enjoy each bite.

5 After you have finished your breakfast, record what you had to eat in your journal. Then record your thoughts and feelings about the experience. How was this different from the normal way you eat breakfast? Was it more satisfying or less satisfying? Do you feel full or hungry? Did you eat more slowly than usual? What did you like about eating mindfully? Did any emotions come up? Did you feel happy, sad, frustrated? If so, write about how the experience made you feel and anything else that comes to mind.

PART TWO

YOUR RELATIONSHIP WITH FOOD

Since you were a baby you have had an intimate and complex relationship with food. Your family, your parents, the patterns you have developed over the years, the influence of the food industry, have all shaped what, how and why you eat today. Your relationship with food may be unsatisfactory and troubled, yet you may not know all the reasons why that is so. To heal your relationship with food you need to examine the sources of your distress.

WHY YOU STRUGGLE WITH FOOD & WEIGHT

◆

When practising the Mindfulness Diet, it is important to understand your current relationship with food, so you can better understand how it has been serving or not serving you. At the present moment, because you are reading this book, you may be aware that you are in trouble with food. You may sometimes feel out of control with your eating, so that you find it difficult to stop eating foods that you know are unhealthy. Once you start eating, say, a large packet of crisps or pizza, you may find it impossible to eat a normal portion or you may eat the whole thing. Emotional eating may be playing a part in your addiction to food — you may discover you have been suppressing old pain by overeating ice cream, chocolates or crisps.

I N PART II of this book we will explore how emotional eating may be causing you to overindulge and eat unhealthy foods. We will also look at how addictions to salt, sugar and fat can play a part in your eating habits. Food manufacturers and restaurants create foods that intentionally combine salts, sugars and fats in ways that are addictive to the human brain. This may help to guarantee that you buy a certain product again or return to their restaurant, but it does not help you to live a healthy life. These unhealthy, sugary, salty, fat-laden foods are marketed in ways that are seductive and enticing, and you are exposed to these advertisements continually. Many of these foods are filled with chemicals and poor-quality fats.

Restaurant portions have grown over the past decades, adding to the problem of overeating and obesity. In addition, there are other considerations, such as how food production affects the earth and our environment. Examining how you eat also plays a part in sorting out your current relationship with food. You may live a very busy life, so finding time to have a leisurely, healthy meal may seem impossible. Yet eating breakfast whilst standing at the sink, wolfing down lunch at a cafe or hastily eating ready-prepared dinners with your family may be contributing to your dysfunctional relationship with food. Part of healing this relationship may involve reconnecting with the acts of food preparation and eating. As you will discover, having a healthy, mindful, conscious meal may have more to do with habit than with lack of time.

Feeling Out of Control with Food

There is a connection between eating without awareness and feeling out of control with food. You may eat alone late at night, or snack constantly out of your desk drawer at work. If you are having trouble with food addictions, you may not remember everything you eat in a particular day. You may block out the fact that you have binged on ice cream, or eaten a large pizza when you weren't hungry. When you feel a craving arise, you may feel that you have to have whatever it is you are craving, and single-mindedly go in pursuit of it.

Simply knowing you will soon satisfy your craving will calm your addictive anxiety when it arises. You may tell yourself that tomorrow you will get back on your diet, or that you will never do this again, but you know deep down that you are lying to yourself. You know that tomorrow you will do the same thing over again – just one more time.

Of course, feeling out of control with food fosters feelings of shame. You imagine that you are unique in having these problems, but rest assured you are not alone. The complex problem of being overweight or obese often involves feelings of being helpless when it comes to food cravings. This is a result of a combination of negative realities coming together, making it difficult to control eating.

The stress of daily life may be helping you to turn to food as a way to calm your nerves. If you feel out of control with your food, consider whether you are under heavy stress. Beginning to unravel your relationship with food often involves every aspect of your life. If stress is overwhelming you – because of a financial problems, fear of losing your job or lack of support in your family – you may want to write about it in your journal. Writing about each issue that is bothering you will help you feel less overwhelmed.

Take a few moments now to write about how stress may be driving you to overeat and to have food cravings and addictions. Try to answer these questions in your journal and remember to be kind to yourself as you do:

- What are the main causes of stress in my life?
- What foods do I use to relieve the feelings of anxiety when they arise?
- Do I sometimes feel powerless over my cravings and out of control with food?

THE CHILDHOOD VOICES IN YOUR HEAD

Overeating can stem from things you learnt in your childhood or events that happened to you in your childhood. Sometimes hurtful things said to you when you were a child by a thoughtless parent, or other adult family member, can leave long-lasting scars. Maybe your father told you that you were too fat in front of his friends. Perhaps your mother was, for whatever reason, not able to nurture you or make you feel secure and loved. These experiences can become etched in your psyche. Unfortunately, you may be overeating in order to drown out these painful feelings from your past.

MANY PEOPLE use food to bury their emotions, whether these are from the past or the present. If you are having emotional difficulties with your spouse or other loved ones, or your boss, or simply having difficulty coping with daily life, then you may be overeating, or eating unhealthy foods, to compensate. Becoming mindful of the emotional reasons you eat is an important step to healing your relationship with food. Writing in your journal is a good place to start.

EXERCISE 4

IDENTIFYING EMOTIONAL TRIGGERS

Consider the following in order to find a connection between your emotions and your eating habits:

• **Find time where you can be alone and undisturbed.** Record in your journal anything that was said or happened to you in your childhood that you feel may be connected to problems with food you are having today. Making the link between these past hurts and your current problems with food is a big step towards healing.

• **Try to remember the last time you used food to calm your emotions, then write about it.** You may have felt angry with your boss for making unrealistic demands. So, you came home from work and ate a large pizza while watching TV. See if you can make the connection between emotions, stress and eating, and how the events are interlinked.

• **Write down five things you could do when you are emotionally upset instead of overeating.** These will help you deal with your emotions in a positive, self-nurturing way. Try writing in your journal about what is upsetting you, meditate for ten minutes when you get home, or take a hot bath or ask your partner for a massage.

HOW PROCESSED FOODS CAUSE OVEREATING

◆

Now that you have explored some of the emotional reasons behind eating, it's time to examine what you eat — and how your food choices could be contributing to your problems with your weight. To start, we need to look at processed foods.

UNTIL THE EARLY 1800s, people in Western countries ate produce out of their gardens, or bought foods that were fresh and locally grown. Eggs came from the chickens in the hen house, and animals were more humanely raised: chickens were free to run around the garden, and cows grazed in the pasture. When the time came for slaughter, it was done humanely. Chemicals and chemical preservatives, antibiotics, hormones, flavourisers and texturisers now routinely added to our foods were unknown. Foods were locally produced and seasonal. People ate hardy greens and cabbages in the spring, fresh tomatoes and peaches in the summer, and apples in the autumn. Vitamin and mineral content of produce was high, and the available food was nourishing. Bottling was popular as a way of preserving fruits and vegetables for winter use.

Food processing is not new and, in fact, dates back to prehistoric ages when foods were preserved by drying, fermenting or salting. These tried-and-tested processing and preserving techniques remained the same until the beginning of the industrial revolution. Then, in the 19th century,

43

modern food-processing technology was invented to serve military needs. In 1809 Nicholas Appert invented vacuum-bottling as a way to supply food for French troops, and British merchant Peter Durand developed the tin can in 1810. Later, pasteurisation, invented by Louis Pasteur in 1862, helped ensure the safety of canned food.

In the 20th century, the migration into cities and a rising consumer society in Western Europe and North America caused an explosion of new food-processing techniques. These included freeze-drying, artificial sweetening, artificial colouring and the use of chemical preservatives. In the second half of the 20th century, processed convenience foods were marketed to middle-class working wives and mothers as time-savers. Food manufacturers introduced ready-prepared meals, as well as frozen foods, and juice concentrates. Food processing and manufacturing has grown to be an extremely profitable industry.

There are some benefits to food processing. For example, toxins can be removed, consistency can be maintained, and marketing and distribution is easier. In addition, seasonal foods are now available year round. Modern supermarkets would not exist without modern food-processing techniques. Processed foods are often less susceptible to early spoilage than fresh foods, and are better suited for long-distance travel from the source to the consumer. As individuals, we may benefit from the convenience of having a range of foods readily available. The reality is that more and more of us live in cities far away from where food is grown. In many of our families the adults work away from home, so a fully prepared ready-to-eat meal that can be heated up in the microwave in a few minutes seems attractive. Grabbing a box or packet of something from the grocery store shelves is quick and easy, but it may also offer a clue in understanding the rising rates of obesity mentioned in Part I. The drawbacks of processed foods definitely outnumber the benefits.

In general, fresh food contains a higher proportion of naturally occurring vitamins, fibre and minerals than an equivalent product processed by the food industry. Vitamin C, for example, is destroyed by heat, and therefore canned fruits have a lower content of vitamin C than fresh ones. Food processing can lower the nutritional value of foods, and introduce hazards not encountered with naturally occurring products. The food additives used, such as chemical flavourings and texture-enhancing agents, have no nutritive value, and can be unhealthy. In addition, chemical preservatives added or created during processing to extend the 'shelf life' of commercial food products such as nitrites or sulphites, may have adverse health effects. Then there is the use of low-cost ingredients that mimic the properties of natural ingredients, such as trans fats – cheap, chemically hardened vegetable oils – in place of more expensive, natural saturated fats or cold-pressed oils. These have been shown to cause severe health problems, including

> Avoid food products containing ingredients that
> no ordinary human would keep in the pantry.
> Ethoxylated diglycerides? Cellulose? Xanthan gum?
> Calcium propionate? Ammonium sulphate? If you
> wouldn't cook with them yourself, why let others
> use these ingredients to cook for you?
>
> MICHAEL POLLAN, AUTHOR & FOOD ACTIVIST

heart disease, but are still in widespread use. Most importantly, processed foods often have a higher ratio of calories to other essential nutrients than unprocessed foods, a phenomenon referred to as 'empty calories'. So-called 'junk foods' are most often mass-produced, processed food products.

So, what does this have to do with the problems you may have with overeating and obesity? First, eating processed foods made of empty calories starves the body of good nutrition, and at the same time introduces harmful chemicals and additives to your body. Because processed foods are often nutrient-poor, you will feel less satisfaction and fulfilment when eating them. This contributes to the desire to eat more as your body tries in vain to find the nutrition that is just not there. In addition new ways of making food 'highly palatable', with strategic combinations of salt, fat and sugar, encourages overeating (see pages 49–51). Once you start eating them, these highly palatable combinations can become addictive.

Profit drives most aspects of any industry, the food industry included. In much of the food industry, health concerns are generally subservient to profit motive, leading many companies to ignore major health concerns raised by the use of chemical ingredients. Only through consumer pressure has there been a reduction in the use of some of these ingredients – trans fats, for example. As consumers, we need to give up the idea that the food industry has our health and well-being at heart. Instead, we can take back our health through mindfully paying attention to the quality and wholesomeness of the food we eat, and making better individual choices in our diet.

FOOD ADDICTIONS & YOUR BRAIN

◆

For thousands of years, human weight remained relatively stable. For the hundred years prior to the 1980s, since most people were of a normal size, scientists assumed human beings were 'programmed' to eat no more than they needed to remain at a stable, healthy weight. In other words it was thought that your body and brain know automatically how much to eat to match how many calories you burn.

I N 1994 a study published by Katherine Flegal, of the US Centers for Disease Control and Prevention, showed a very dramatic increase in the rate of obesity in the USA since the 1980s. Flegal was shocked to discover that one-third of the

population was overweight. Since that study, Flegal has continued to track the growing weight of Americans. In 1960 women between the ages of 20 to 29 averaged 58 kg (9 st 2 lb). In a study taken in 2000, the average weight of women in the same age group was 71 kg (11 st 3 lb). Flegal also discovered that those who were overweight were more likely to continue to gain.

During the 1970s and 80s food became more readily available. Fast-food chains expanded, portion sizes grew, new packaged and processed foods filled grocery shelves, and out-of-season food began to be shipped in from all over the world. But these factors alone do not explain why so many people now struggle with food addictions and cravings. Why is it that a large portion of the population is suddenly having issues with willpower, lack of self-esteem and out-of-control eating? Even those who manage to keep their weight down still find themselves having food cravings.

The answer may be that the foods we are now eating are stimulating the reward areas of the brain, which are overriding the natural wisdom of the body to control weight. As humans we are programmed to pursue pleasure because it is essential to our survival. We pursue those things that make us feel good – sex and food, for example – and avoid those things that threaten us or make us feel bad – such as pain, a wild bear on the prowl, a dangerous part of town or tainted food. When we anticipate a reward we are motivated to act – in this case to eat. Unfortunately, we are eating foods designed to make us overeat.

Much of what the food industry has provided us in recent decades are foods that are strategically designed to be 'highly palatable'. Highly palatable foods combine sugar, fat and salt in ways that are not found in nature – and that overstimulate the reward centres of the brain. And so, we go back for more...

ADDICTIVE COMBINATIONS

Restaurant and fast-food chains deliberately design foods for high palatability, using the reward-centre triggers of salt, fat and sugar. Menus are developed so that you will be tempted to overeat and, hopefully, develop a craving for whatever it is they are serving and return for more. The combination has to be just right – not too sugary, not too salty, not too greasy. Industry insiders refer to this combination as the 'bliss point'.

SOME EXAMPLES OF FOODS that combine salt, fat and sugar in ways that promote overeating may be items you recognise from restaurant menus: when you eat at restaurants or order takeaway, how often do you choose the following?

• Creamy milkshakes.
• Salads dressed with high-calorie dressings made with salt, fat and sugars.
• Fried foods served with honey dipping sauces.

- Chips made with salt and trans fats.
- Beefburgers served on buns made of refined white flour.
- Puddings made with sugars, refined flours and fats, such as pies, cakes, cheesecake, doughnuts, cookies or pastries.
- Ice cream that contains a large proportion of high-fat cream, sugars and chemical additives.
- Pizza made with refined flour, fatty cheeses, salty sausage and sweetened tomato sauce.
- Coffee drinks made with whipped cream and sugar.

In grocery stores, many processed foods also artfully combine salt, fat and sugar to up the addiction ante. They include:

- Breakfast cereals made with refined flours, sugars and fats.
- Boxed biscuits that are high in fat, high in sugar and made with refined flours.
- High-calorie chocolate bars that are rich in fats and sugars.
- Packaged convenience foods that have a high-fat, high-sugar and high-salt content.
- Frozen pizzas made with refined flour, fatty cheeses and meats, and sugary tomato sauce.
- Ready-prepared meals made with trans fats, salt and sugars.
- Low-calorie/low-fat foods that are high in sugar and salt.
- Breads made of refined flour, sugars and fats with chemical additives for long shelf-life.
- Artificially sweetened foods that are high in fats and salt.

- Corn and potato crisps made with fats and salt.
- Creamy dips for use with corn or potato crisps.
- Packaged snacks of all kinds, both savoury and sweet.

Eating foods high in salt, fat and sugar makes us want to eat more foods high in salt, fat and sugar. The more 'bliss-engineered' foods we eat, the more we want them. Having greater access to these foods in the last decades has over-stimulated the reward centres in our brains, and increased our cravings and addictions. This all goes to show that the cards really are stacked against us when it comes to controlling weight. Through mindfulness, and knowledge of healthy eating, we can begin to reclaim a healthy relationship with food. A return to simple, natural whole foods is the answer.

Over-consumption of Meat

For your personal health and well-being, consider cutting back on meat and dairy. It is not necessary to become a vegetarian, but reducing the amount of animal protein in your diet will improve your health. As a species we are omnivores. Many of us are used to eating meat, but meat consumption has risen over the past decades in both the Western and developing countries, along with diseases associated with increased intake of saturated fats. The increased caloric intake has also led to increased obesity.

Diets that are high in animal protein and saturated fat have been shown to increase the risk of both heart disease and cancer. Red meat in particular has been linked with higher incidence of heart disease, prostate cancer, breast cancer and colon cancer. In addition, too much animal protein can put a strain on your liver and kidneys; it can also promote osteoporosis, because when your body excretes too much protein it excretes too much calcium along with it.

> Moving to a more plant-based diet is one personal thing you can do to help save the planet.

That juicy beefburger or steak may be hard to give up, even when you know the health risks. Knowing the facts about eating meat and the effects of meat consumption on the environment may give you extra motivation to cut down. Here is a laundry list of reasons to eat fewer animal and dairy products:

• Your grocery bill will be lower if you eat more grains, vegetables, fruits, nuts and pulses and less meat, dairy and processed junk foods.

• You don't need meat to live. So you can be perfectly healthy eating smaller amounts of it.

• The majority of meat and dairy comes from factory farms, a large proportion of which use inhumane methods of raising and slaughtering animals.

• Antibiotic usage, contamination of both land and water by

A study by the National Institutes of Health–American Association of Retired Persons published in 2009 in the *Archives of Internal Medicine* reported the findings from half-a-million people that the consumption of red meat was significantly associated with increases in total mortality, cardiovascular mortality and cancer mortality. A recent study published in the *Journal of the American Dietetic Association* showed that LDL cholesterol (the bad cholesterol) and inflammation (a risk factor for heart disease) worsened on a diet that was high in animal protein and improved significantly on a low-fat, whole-food, plant-based diet.

fertilisers used to produce feed, the use of pesticides and herbicides for feed crops, the clearing of forests for land on which to raise livestock and excessive water usage all have a huge impact on the environment.

• Raising livestock produces more greenhouse gases than the emissions from all transportation combined. Greenhouse gases are known to contribute to global warming.

• If you move away from beef and pork towards chicken, fish and eggs you decrease your personal contribution to greenhouse gases significantly.

• More moderate meat consumption worldwide will lead to lower meat production, less inhumane animal treatment, reduced amounts of greenhouse gases.

FOOD MARKETING PROMOTES OBESITY

◆

Food advertising and marketing works by cueing brain circuits that lead you to overeat. In a study published in 2009 in Health Psychology, *Yale University researchers showed two groups of children a cartoon, one with food ads and one without, and provided snacks. The children watching the food ads ate 45 per cent more than the other group. It wasn't just the children who were affected – adults who watched a programme with food ads also ate more than those who watched one without them. This was particularly true for men and for people who were trying to diet. Most of us would like to believe that food advertising does not influence us. Studies such as the one at Yale show that we are in fact heavily influenced. There is a reason why the food advertising industry is worth millions of pounds. It works.*

YALE RESEARCHER Jennifer L. Harris confirms that people are snacking more than they used to, which rebuts food industry claims that the ads influence only brand selection. Her studies show that food advertising makes people eat whatever is available, not just the foods that are advertised.

In the supermarkets, packaging emblazoned with attractive food photography and seductive copy entices you to try a product. And, of course, there is a dizzying array of products to choose from. When you get home and sit in front of the TV, you may see an ad depicting a beautiful women, in what appears to be a state of bliss, eating a chocolate pudding. Between

your favourite shows, you will be enticed with a succulent-looking beefburger or a pizza oozing with melted cheese. Even if you were not hungry, these ads may be enough to make you want to drive back to the shop or restaurant and indulge.

Food ads appear everywhere: in magazines, on buses and billboards, on TV and radio. Large posters of the latest specials are placed prominently in the windows of fast-food chains. It's hard to avoid overeating when you are inundated day and night by images of highly palatable foods.

In the USA, the Food Channel, a cable TV channel that shows cooking shows non-stop 24 hours a day, offers constant stimulation to the brain circuits that cue the desire to eat. In the UK, cooking shows with celebrity chefs function in the same way. Interestingly in both the USA and the UK the rising popularity of cooking shows mirrors the growing obsession with food, and parallels the rising rates of obesity.

The surge in cooking shows is a complicated issue. There is nothing wrong with learning to cook well – cooking is an important aspect of eating mindfully. Many of the shows make use of fresh ingredients and promote healthy eating. That said, others focus on the foods that are highly palatable combinations of fat, salt and sugar. Watching these shows adds to the external influences that make it hard to avoid overeating. Watching a celebrity chef make a decadent chocolate cake or a potato dish laden with cheese and cream makes you want to make it yourself, and gives subtle permission for you to do so.

EXERCISE 5

BECOMING MINDFUL OF WHY I EAT

This exercise can be done in a day, but is more effective if done over a period of a week. The idea is to record why you are eating every time you eat something. Record whatever you drink as well, again listing the reason. You will find it easier to do this if you carry a small notebook in your handbag or pocket: that way you can jot down your thoughts wherever you are. Later you can transfer the information you collect to your journal.

WRITE DOWN EVERYTHING you eat during the day, even if it is just a bite, and any reason why you decided to eat at that time. You may not have made a clear decision to eat but just mindlessly grabbed for a snack. Note that as well. Sometimes you may not be sure why you decided to eat; write that down. Beginning to pay attention in this way will help you to become more mindful of what triggers your eating habits. If you become aware of why you eat, every time you eat, you can begin gradually to shift away from overeating and eating unhealthy foods. Make sure you write down any sugary, high-calorie drinks that may be undermining your efforts to control overeating.

The following reasons are some suggestions of why you might eat. They may not be logical or rational, and may even be contradictory:

- It is a mealtime and I'm hungry.
- It is a mealtime and I'm not hungry but I eat anyway.
- I'm nervous or anxious about something.
- I'm bored.
- I am craving sugar or carbohydrates.
- I am craving a beefburger.
- I am craving a particular food or snack.
- I feel a need for caffeine or a stimulant.
- I was drawn to eat something because of its packaging.
- I was snacking whilst watching TV or surfing the Internet.
- I ate at a restaurant with friends.
- I ate at a restaurant alone.
- I was in a supermarket that offers free samples.
- I was angry, sad or afraid, and ate for comfort.
- I saw an ad for food and it made me hungry.
- I watched a cooking show and it made me hungry.
- I ate whilst driving in my car.
- I ate snacks at my desk at work.
- I wanted something sweet and creamy.
- I needed to eat when watching TV.
- I felt tired.
- I was craving something salty.
- I wanted a sugary fizzy drink.
- I wanted an alcoholic drink.
- I snacked as I cooked dinner.
- I was hungry at bedtime.

EXERCISE 6

BECOMING MINDFUL OF THE AMOUNT I EAT

This exercise builds on the last one. Again, you are going to write down everything you eat for a day, but this time you are going to focus on the amount you are eating. Studies have shown that when participants are asked to record faithfully everything they have eaten for a period of time, they consistently underestimate portions, so it is important to be clear about portion size before you begin.

To counteract the tendency to underestimate portion sizes, use the following guide to judge what you have eaten. Note the non-starchy vegetables you eat, but don't worry about the amounts.

• A sandwich should be the size of two decks of playing cards arranged side-by-side.

• A portion of rice should be no larger than a light bulb.

• A jacket potato should be the size of the palm of your hand.

• A serving of chocolate should be no larger than a packet of dental floss.

• A serving of meat should be no larger than a deck of playing cards.

• A serving of pasta should be the size of a cricket ball.

• A dollop of salad dressing should be no larger than the size of a two-pound coin.

• A serving of fish should be no larger than the size of two decks of playing cards.

• A serving of chips should be the size of a cricket ball.

• A serving of sliced cold meats should be the size of a DVD.

• A serving of nuts should be the size of a golf ball.

• A serving of cheese should be no larger than three dice.

• A serving of butter should be the size of a two-pound coin.

• A serving of cereal should be the size of a cricket ball.

• A serving of beans should be the size of a light bulb.

• A serving of biscuits is one medium-sized biscuit.

• A serving of cake should be no larger than a deck of playing cards.

Write down everything you consume in day. At the end of the day look over what you have written. Find an online weight-loss calculator and a reference website that gives the nutrient and calorie content of foods (use an Internet search engine, and enter the terms 'weight-loss calculator' and 'nutrient content of foods' to do this). Use the online weight-loss calculator to work out the amount of calories you need to maintain your current weight (the calculator should take into account your gender, age and height and the amount of exercise that you do) and the reference sites to establish the nutritional value and calorie content of the foods that you ate. Then try to answer the questions on the following page in your journal.

EXERCISE 7

BECOMING MINDFUL OF WHAT FOODS I EAT

Using the information you gathered in the last two exercises, ask yourself the following questions:

• Did I eat any vegetables? Were they fresh, canned or frozen?
• Did I eat any fruit? Was it fresh, frozen or canned?
• How much meat did I eat? How much dairy did I eat?
• Which foods, if any, were high in saturated fat?
• Were any of the foods I ate sugary puddings?
• Were any of the foods ready-prepared, refined or processed?
• Did any of the foods I eat contain preservatives or chemical additives?

Mindfulness practice is the key to becoming conscious of what you eat and why you eat it. It will help you to intervene in negative habitual eating patterns that are wreaking havoc on your health and your weight. Most importantly it will help you to pay closer attention to the quality of the food you are eating so that you can begin to move towards a more healthy diet. Cutting down on any foods with unnatural combinations of salt, fat, sugar, preservatives and chemicals, and replacing them with delicious, beautifully prepared natural whole foods will restore sanity and balance to your eating. Mindfulness practice is the first step towards healing your relationship with food.

EATING ON THE RUN,
EATING ROUND THE CLOCK

◆

In modern times, food is available 24 hours a day, and eating at all times, day or night, is acceptable. Snacking throughout the day is easy to do as food is available everywhere – in shops, the fridge, fast-food restaurants, coffee houses, vending machines, your desk drawer at work. Supermarkets are open late, and a meal can be just a micro-wave away. It is common practice to bring muffins, cakes and biscuits into work. Quick-fix food products – such as power bars or protein shakes – are sold for 'energy' at yoga and fitness centres, even though these so-called health foods often have a high-fat and high-sugar content. The same goes for sugary athletic drinks.

EATING IRREGULARLY, at any time of day or night, combined with eating whilst on the move is a recipe for unhealthy eating. We may have good intentions to keep to a schedule of a normal breakfast, lunch and dinner, but often there is not enough time for breakfast in the morning, meetings can often run late and meals end up being taken at odd times during the day. Eating whilst driving, commuting or on a short break at work is common and acceptable (although not very safe when it comes to driving). The lack of regular family meals, the pressures and stresses of work and the general hyperactivity of modern urban living contributes to 'eating round the clock' and 'eating on the run' syndromes.

Becoming mindful of these syndromes can help to return a sense of control and sanity to your relationship with food. For the next few days, try to follow a regular eating schedule. Eat three meals and two small snacks – one taken between breakfast and lunch and one between lunch and your evening meal. The snacks should be a piece of fruit, a handful of nuts or some carrot sticks – something very light, fresh and simple. Avoid eating at other times or after dinner. Avoid snacks set out at work, or raiding the refrigerator in the evening. Begin to get used to regular meal times, and get your body used to eating on a schedule. You will be glad you did.

LIVING ALONE & EATING ALONE

One of the realities of modern urban life is that many people live alone. Solo living can have its joys – not having to argue with anyone about dishes in the sink, not sharing the bathroom in the morning, and simply having peace and quiet after work. However, living alone also has its downside, and that can be a sense of loneliness – one of the big triggers for overeating.

COOKING FOR ONE may bring up any sense of loneliness you feel about living on your own. Meals may be taken in front of the TV where the distraction of your favourite show may cause you not to notice what or how much you are eating. It may seem like too much work to make a proper balanced meal; an entire large packet of chips, a bottle of salsa and a glass of wine may suffice, or you may make do with something from the fridge popped into the microwave. Not the best nutrition, and not terribly enjoyable.

Food can be a powerful symbol of love, family, marriage, nourishment, joy, friendship, nurturing, survival, happiness, pleasure, health and even wealth. When you eat alone in a mindless way, those emotional and symbolic meanings may be evoked but then immediately buried if you feel that you are missing those things in your life. In order to avoid feeling bereft, you may unconsciously overeat or eat unhealthy foods.

Even if you live with someone else, you may eat alone in restaurants for some or all your meals. You may need to eat out because of your work schedule or because you travel for your work. Or you simply may be lost when it comes to cooking if the person who tends to do the cooking in your home is away. Eating out alone on a regular basis can spark feelings of loneliness or other emotions that cause overeating. In addition, restaurant servings tend to be large, and these oversized portions may quickly begin to seem like the norm.

Eating out alone on a regular basis can spark feelings of loneliness or other emotions that cause overeating.

There is nothing inherently wrong with eating alone, of course. However, unless it is practised with mindfulness, it can hinder you from maintaining a healthy weight and/or a healthy body. That said, each person is different. Eating alone may not be a problem for some, but a problem for others. The best way to see how eating alone affects you is to begin to pay attention to how you feel, and what you eat, when you do. For one week record in your notebook every time you eat alone. Ask yourself the following questions:

• How did I feel when eating on my own? Was I happy, sad, lonely or not really aware of how I was feeling?
• Did I eat at home or in a restaurant?
• If at home, did I cook a healthy meal for myself or eat a meal of less than healthy snack food?
• What did I eat if I ate in a restaurant? Did I make healthy food choices?
• Did I overeat when I ate alone?

Becoming mindful of how you feel and eat when dining alone will help you identify any negative patterns you may need to address. If you know you will be eating alone, find creative ways to intervene and make dining solo an enjoyable experience.

EATING WITH OTHERS

◆

Eating with others can be enjoyable, nurturing and nourishing. However, like eating alone, it can sometimes be a trigger for overeating. The practice of mindfulness can help you to determine whether eating with others affects your relationship to food.

AFTER EATING A MEAL with friends or family, and the dishes are done or you've returned home from the restaurant, take some time to reflect on how you felt during the meal and how your emotions affected your eating. Try to answer the following questions in your journal:

• Did eating with my friend(s) or family cause me to eat more or less?

• Did others impact on the amount that I ate, and why?

• Did the person or people I was eating with encourage me to have more than I normally would?

• Was I comfortable with the person or people I was with, or did I experience tension or difficult emotions?

• Did I feel the person or persons I was eating with judged either what I ate or the amount that I ate?

• Do I enjoy eating with other people more than eating on my own? If so why?

• Does food taste better when I eat with other people or on my own?

PART THREE

YOUR OWN MINDFULNESS DIET

The Mindfulness Diet brings the ancient practice of mindfulness to bear on a difficult and painful problem – your personal struggle to relate to food in a healthy way. It puts your struggles in the larger context of the growing obesity epidemic and the changing way that food is produced and distributed. Through practising mindfulness, learning to be present to yourself, and confronting the fact that certain kinds of foods are unhealthy and addictive, you can turn an unconscious out-of-control relationship to food to one that is based on knowledge, self-love, enjoyment and good health.

FORGING A NEW RELATIONSHIP WITH FOOD

◆

What you eat, why you eat and how you eat affects how you feel and function as you go through your day. The Mindfulness Diet will help you deepen your consciousness about how important food is to your health and well-being. Before you build your personalised Mindfulness Diet, it is important to learn the traditional mindfulness meditations on the body, the mind and the emotions.

P RACTISING THESE MEDITATIONS on a daily basis will help you bring the increased self-awareness you will enjoy to your relationship with food you eat.

Through the practice of mindfulness, you will be able to heal your relationship to food, normalise your weight, enjoy better health, enhance your mood and energy, and perhaps even increase your longevity. The Mindfulness Diet is not one of those short-term diets that promises 'X' amount of weight loss. It is a way of life built on kindness to yourself and the world around you.

Before we begin to build our personalised Mindfulness Diet, we will spend some time exploring mindfulness practices, so we can better bring these 'tools' to bear on our relationship to our bodies and the food we eat. This may seem like a detour, but deepening your ability to feel and pay attention is essential to healing your relationship with food. It is the doorway to restoring real pleasure and joy to everyday

eating. Buddhists have spent thousands of years perfecting the art of paying attention, so what better way to learn mindfulness than from the master himself – the Buddha?

A Deeper Exploration of Mindfulness Practice

Buddhists have practised mindfulness meditation for thousands of years. Mindfulness meditation begins with a calm stable mind, often achieved with focusing on the breath, which you learned in Part I. You work with the calm, stable mind you have cultivated to investigate your body, feelings and attitudes, your mind and your thoughts, and the physical world around you.

Mindfulness is dedication to observing and seeing clearly, and being conscious and aware of what is happening in the present moment. Mindfulness helps you gain a deeper understanding of the connection between your thoughts and feelings, and how they manifest in your actions related to eating. Mindfulness practice can be transformative. You begin to observe yourself and see who you are, how you act, what you feel and what you think when it comes to food. You begin to know yourself in a different and deeper way than your normal way of perceiving yourself. The fog of unconsciousness lifts, and you begin to make good choices for yourself, so that eating becomes a healthy, pleasurable activity.

Buddhists have spent thousands of years perfecting the art of paying attention...

Mindfulness meditation leads naturally to the examination of things you may think of as fixed or unchangeable, such as your personality and your habits around food and eating. Not realising you have the ability to change, you may continue each day being trapped in habitual thoughts and behaviour around food and eating – even though these are not serving you. Through mindfulness practice, you can begin to recognise your patterns and choose a better alternative.

YOU & YOUR BODY

Some spiritual traditions teach that you must ignore the body and move towards a more spiritual approach to life where you identify exclusively with the mind. The body may be considered as defiled and a source of 'sin', to be neglected and ignored. It does not require a great stretch of the imagination to think that overeating and ignoring the physical sensations may have its roots in some of these traditions.

W E ARE INCARNATED in our human bodies. Our body enables us to communicate, to work, to love, to experience joy, to eat, to sleep and to take care of ourselves. Rather than being an enemy, our bodies are a source of pleasure, joy and inspiration as well as spiritual development. Through our bodies we appreciate the world around us.

It is important to learn to pay attention to our bodies, to care for them well and to stay in balance physically and mentally. Becoming mindful of our body will help us reconnect if we have been disconnected from our physical sensations through trauma or abuse. Mindfulness can help us release the past so as to live more fully in the present.

Rather than being an enemy, our bodies are a source of pleasure, joy and inspiration.

Since the body and mind are not separate, awareness of the body also provides a window into our psychological states. The pain in the neck, the tensed jaw, the tightness in the chest, may point to areas of our psyche that need exploration and healing. Eating beyond fullness is easy to do if you are cut off from feeling your body fully. Focusing closely on your body will help you release areas of 'armouring' you may not have been aware of, and will open you to moving through the psychological blocks these areas may represent. This can be an important step on the pathway to normalising and healing your relationship to food.

EXERCISE 8

MINDFULNESS OF BODY

Set aside about 30 minutes for this exercise, choosing a time when you can be undisturbed. If possible, record the instructions for this exercise so that you can play them back to yourself.

1 Sit on a straight-backed chair with both feet on the floor and your hands resting in your lap. Sit a little forwards on the seat and do not lean against the chair back. You should feel upright but relaxed, as if a string attached to the top of your head is holding you up from above.

2 With your eyes closed or slightly open, relax any tense areas of your body. Calm your mind by focusing on your breath for a few minutes as it passes over your upper lip.

3 Now, shift your focus from your breath to your feet. Be aware of any physical sensations in your feet, and relax any tensions that may be present. Then move your awareness to your ankles, lower legs and knees and do the same. Next, move on to your thighs and notice any feelings you may have here. Notice any sensations such as feelings of wanting to move, tension, tingling. Do you feel tightness, burning or an ache? Try to remain neutral and detached. Just be aware. Focus completely on that sensation without labelling it 'pleasant' or 'unpleasant'. If there is pain, simply note that there is pain.

4 Now move on to your groin area and stomach area. Relax and let your breath fill your lower abdomen. Breathe into your lower abdomen for a minute or two, and then move your awareness into your mid and upper chest area.

5 Next, focus on your neck, letting go of any tension in this area. When ready, move your attention to your face. Relax every part of your face – your mouth, eyes, jaw and forehead.

6 Now move your attention to more subtle sensations. Focus on your heart beating in your chest for a few minutes. Then expand your awareness to your veins and arteries connecting to your heart, and try to feel the blood pumping through them. Notice if your heart slows down or speeds up as you do this.

7 Focus on the general feeling of energy moving through your body. Feel energy moving around your spine and through your torso and in your groin area. Stay with neutral observation, avoiding labelling anything 'positive' or 'negative'.

8 Shift your attention to your senses. What are you seeing at this moment, tasting or smelling? What colours do you notice? Pay attention to what you hear. Simply listen to the sounds near and far, as well as the sound of your breath.

9 Return to focusing on your breath. Meditate for a few minutes before ending this exercise.

Body Mindfulness & Food

What does this body mindfulness exercise have to do with food? Often, having trouble with food in your life stems from a lack of connection to the body. When you practise feeling your body again, this helps you to distinguish real hunger from emotional hunger. It helps you to recognise when you are tense and thus take steps to address your tension by writing in your journal, exercising, taking a bath or calling a friend – instead of reaching for, say, a tub of ice cream. Body mindfulness allows you to begin the process of undoing any body 'armouring' that has been created from old physical or emotional wounds – the wounds that may be causing you to overeat and abuse your body with unhealthy foods.

Practise body mindfulness when you notice that you are feeling disconnected with your body, having trouble with eating or taking care of yourself physically, or when you simply want to experience your body in a new and beneficial way. Once you are used to closely attending to your body through mindfulness meditation, you can bring the same attention to your body in daily life. You can extend your body awareness to everyday activities such as walking, eating, speaking, driving and observing the world through your senses.

By paying close attention to your body, you will learn more about your physical patterns and habits, change those which are harmful or negative, be conscious of subtle changes that may indicate illness and be better able to maintain your health

and well-being. You will begin to know when you are truly hungry, and when you have eaten enough for your body's needs. You will know, through how your body feels, whether certain foods are healthy for you or problematic.

YOU & YOUR EMOTIONS

Before practising mindfulness of emotions, it is helpful to explore how emotions come into being. First there is some kind of sensory stimulus or thought, which then becomes a basis for a feeling to arise. For example, your partner arrives home early from work. You may experience pleasure at seeing him or her, or you have an immediate sense of fear because you know that there are redundancies in the offing. Or you may feel anxiety because things have not been going well between you for some time. Your partner arriving home is the basis for your feelings to arise.

FEELINGS AND ATTITUDES are often a stimulus to action. Pleasure at seeing your partner may lead you to suggest that you have a cup of coffee and talk. If you feel threatened, you may let your partner stand there, feeling uncomfortable as he or she delivers the bad news. If anger arises, you may say something you later regret. Usually the whole sequence of events – a feeling that gives rise to an attitude (or vice versa) that gives rise to an action – is experienced seamlessly, and feels a part of us.

If you are used to eating when you feel any strong emotion, you may do so in a similar seamless fashion – without even thinking about what you are doing. For example, if your partner suddenly loses his or her job, you may overeat or drink too much in the days that follow to calm down the anxiety you feel. Even if your partner has happened to come home early for no particular reason, the relief you may feel at realising nothing bad has happened may still lead you to eat one of the chocolate bars you keep in the kitchen cupboard.

In mindfulness meditation, you learn to pay close attention to your feelings and to avoid any tendency to repress or suppress them. There is nothing wrong with your emotions – it is natural for you to feel anger, sadness, fear and so on. The problem is when you identify strongly with a particular emotional state. For example, you may think 'I am angry' or 'I am depressed' rather than removing the 'I' and simply acknowledging, that, yes, there is anger, there is sadness or there is fear. Through practising mindfulness, you can begin to observe your anger (or any other emotion) without judgement. You will learn that emotions can arise, linger and pass away, and that you don't have to get caught up in them, or compulsively express them in a way that may be destructive to yourself or to others. You can avoid eating to push feelings down or take away any pain you may be feeling. You learn that your feeling represents a snapshot of where you are at this moment, and – importantly – that feelings naturally change over time.

EXERCISE 9

MINDFULNESS OF EMOTIONS

For this exercise you will need a straight-backed chair. Ensure you are sitting comfortably without using the back of the chair for support.

1 Begin by focusing on your breath. Do this for a few minutes to calm and clear your mind.

2 Choose either a personal situation or a person that you know as your focus for the exercise. Create in your mind a vivid mental image of this situation or person with as much detail as possible. As you contemplate the image, let any feelings arise and note what attitude accompanies them. It is OK if your attitude is positive or negative. Try not to judge yourself.

3 Now shift your attention to your emotional state connected to this situation or person. How are you feeling about it or him or her this moment? Are you happy, sad, afraid or angry? Are you experiencing a combination of emotions? Try to watch your emotional state as an observer without identifying with it.

4 If your emotional state is pleasant, try not to cling to it. If you are sad, try not to push it away. Remind yourself how often your emotional state shifts and how many emotions you have experienced and moved through. Meditate on the fact that all emotional states are impermanent and transitory.

5 Return to meditating on your breath for a few minutes or as long as you wish. Notice how it brings peace and stability to your body and mind. When you are ready, end the exercise.

Unacknowledged emotions can trigger overeating. Becoming mindful of your emotions is a first step towards intervening in unhealthy eating patterns. Assessing your emotional state will help reign in emotional eating. Acknowledge whatever you are feeling and, instead of turning to the fridge, choose a creative way to address your emotions such as writing in your journal or talking to a friend. Remind yourself that everything is impermanent – including your emotions.

Mindfulness is present time awareness. It takes place in the here and now. It is the observance of what is happening right now, in the present moment. It stays forever in the present, surging perpetually on the crest of the ongoing wave of passing time. If you are remembering your second-grade teacher, that is memory. When you then become aware that you are remembering your second-grade teacher that is mindfulness. If you then conceptualize the process and say to yourself, 'Oh, I am remembering', that is thinking.

HENEPOLA GUNARNTANA, SRI LANKAN BUDDHIST MONK

YOU & YOUR MIND

◆

We have explored mindfulness of body and the mindfulness of emotions. Now we will look at the third mindfulness, which is the mindfulness of mind. Here we are working directly with the contents of the mind itself: thoughts, mental images, perceptions, emotions, feelings, memories, fantasies and desires – as they arise and then fall away in a continuous stream.

As you discovered in part i, your mind in its normal state, is somewhat out of control. The chaos of mental activity that takes over your daily life is actually a kind of dream state that is divorced from direct experience of reality. Like most people, your life is filled with patterns and routines. The challenges of your day often take place on the surface of your life, which is filled with things to do and seemingly endless demands from the people around you. Yet you have a choice: to live on the surface, or live your life with depth, as fully present as you are able.

In the first choice you get caught up in one activity after another without much awareness of what is going on with yourself or others. Buddhists call this 'living asleep' or living life as if in a dream. In this state you unconsciously follow a rote pattern with little inner or outer awareness. You are more concerned with yourself, your concerns, your needs and your plans. In this state you will find you are more critical of

yourself, and critical of others. You live in your head, either thinking about a past event, or planning something in the future. In this state you are missing the present.

The second choice is 'living awake'. Through mindfulness of the contents of your mind itself, you can learn to bring yourself into the present. Then you can make better decisions about what to eat, when to eat and how to eat. We begin mindfulness practice by simply observing our thoughts as they enter our awareness and then disappear. We try not to identify with them or get carried away by any one thought.

Instead of simply watching our thoughts, we begin to observe patterns in the content. Is there an emotional tone that repeats such as fear or anger? Do our thoughts seem to drift to money, to health, to food or to sex? Are we either planning for the future or reliving memories? By examining our thoughts we can begin consciously to choose the content of our thoughts, replacing negative thinking patterns with more wholesome and productive ones.

EXERCISE 10

MINDFULNESS OF MIND

You will need a straight-backed chair for this exercise. Refer to the
previous mindfulness exercises for directions on how to sit.

1 Begin by simply observing your breath for a few minutes.
This will calm and clear your mind.

2 Begin to observe the content of your thoughts as they enter
your awareness and then disappear. Try not to identify with or
get carried away by any one thought. Simply observe your
thoughts as a scientist would, from a distance, as he or she
takes notes on their content.

3 After a few minutes begin to observe patterns in the content.
Is there an emotional tone that repeats, such as fear or anger?
Do your thoughts seem to drift to money, to health, to food
or sex? Are you planning for the future or reliving memories?
Try not to judge your thoughts. Accept whatever arises.

4 Notice that by noticing your thoughts you have become
more conscious of them. This gives you a tool for noticing
negative thinking patterns and replacing them with more
positive and helpful ones. If you find yourself constantly worry-
ing about the future, take a moment to breathe into the worry.
Consider that in this present moment, there is nothing to fear.

THE MINDFULNESS DIET BASICS

◆

Learning to pay attention to the content of your thoughts as you go about your day will help you gain control of your life and move it in a more positive direction. With patience and daily practice, you will begin to identify the thought patterns that trigger overeating or encourage you to eat unhealthy foods.

T HE MINDFULNESS DIET is based on learning how to pay attention to your body and mind. The practices you have learnt so far can help you on a daily basis to reconnect to the physical feelings, emotions and thoughts that play a role in unhealthy eating practices. Just as important, the Mindfulness Diet is based on love for yourself and acceptance of where you are at this time in your life. If you are overweight or obese, according to the BMI formula detailed in the introduction, rejoice in the fact that you are taking steps to care for yourself by reading this book and following the Mindfulness Diet.

The rest of this book is about practical ways to make the Mindfulness Diet work for you. It will help you create your own Mindfulness Diet, which will serve you in going forwards for the rest of your life. It is not a short-term quick fix that will help you to, say, fit into a dress for a special event or fit into a swimming costume. Rather, it is a blueprint for self-love and self-care that can help you regain balance and health in your relationship to food now and in the future.

Letting Go of Fear & Shame

One of the roadblocks that prevents you from healing your relationship with food may be a sense of fear and shame about being overweight or out of control with food. You may fear that you will never be able to lose weight. Perhaps you have tried diets in the past, lost weight and then gained it back with a vengeance. You may feel demoralised and have given up hope of reaching a healthy weight, or you may feel shame about being overweight. You may be afraid that others think of you as lacking in willpower, or see you as unattractive. Whatever the reasons for your fear and shame, it is important to let these feelings go.

Using the mindfulness practices you've already learnt to monitor your thinking, begin to track in your journal how often you have negative thoughts about yourself and your relationship to food and your weight. Simply noting this information is the beginning of transforming these unhelpful thoughts into positive and loving ones.

In addition to becoming mindful of negative thinking, one of the best ways to let go of fear and shame is to learn to generate love and compassion for yourself just as you are at this moment. Learning to generate love and compassion for yourself is an empowering and transformative practice that anyone can do. Visualisation is one of the most powerful tools you can use to make changes in your life. It is especially useful when you are trying to make profound changes around food and eating.

EXERCISE 11

VISUALISING SELF-LOVE

The following visualisation exercise will help you to tap into the love and compassion that surrounds you and is part of you. Self-love and compassion is the foundation of the Mindfulness Diet. With self-love and compassion for yourself and others, you can accomplish anything. Try this exercise now to begin to learn to love and care for yourself:

1 Find a comfortable place to sit; choose somewhere you can be alone and undisturbed whilst you carry out this exercise. Close your eyes and breathe deeply into your abdomen for a few minutes. Let yourself relax from head to toe.

2 Now, visualise a loving figure in front of you. That person could be someone or something that you consider to be your higher power: God, Mary, Jesus, Buddha, a goddess figure such as the Buddhist Tara or the Greek Athena, nature or the universe. Alternatively, you could choose someone you trust in your personal life such as a family member, a beloved teacher, a therapist or a dear friend.

3 Imagine that person smiling at you, communicating with their eyes and their whole being that they love you unconditionally and want you to be free from suffering and any feelings of fear and shame about your weight and your relationship with food.

4 Now visualise a beam of golden light emanating from their heart and streaming into yours. The light is beautiful, warm and nourishing. Your heart fills with warmth and light as you bask in the feeling of being loved and accepted as you are. The fear and shame evaporates and you feel safe and secure because that person, entity or higher power loves you deeply, exactly as you are right now – with your gifts and talents, flaws and problems, beauty and positive qualities, obsessions and neuroses, food addictions and excess weight. There is nothing about you that you need to split off and reject. He, she or it loves the whole package that is you.

5 When you are ready, thank the being you have visualised and let the image dissolve from your mind's eye. Spend a minute or two imagining the person or being you have visualised as taking up residence in your heart, where he or she is available to you whenever you need encouragement and support in loving and caring for yourself.

6 Open your eyes and breathe deeply for a few moments. If you are so moved, write about your experience in your journal.

Practise this nurturing exercise every morning. If you like, you can ask your higher power for help and guidance during the day. You will find that visualising symbols of love and compassion in this way allows you to tap into your own self-love and compassion – which has been there all along.

EXERCISE 12

IDENTIFYING FIVE PROBLEM FOODS

In our current situation, with the cards stacked against us by the advertising and food industries, it is hard not to have problem foods. Each of us has our own collection of foods that trigger overeating. This exercise offers you a chance to identify your personal problem foods so that you can begin to replace them with healthier choices.

1 Spend a few minutes generating a sense of love for yourself, just as you are, before you start.

2 Begin by making three columns on a blank page in your journal. In the first column list any foods that you feel cause you to overeat, and include any drinks such as beer, cappucino or cola that are problematic for you. How do you identify these foods? These are the ones that you find yourself craving, and the ones that you find it difficult to stop eating; perhaps you binge on them when you are alone. These foods may be amongst your first choices for comfort when you are hungry, or when you are emotionally upset or lonely.

3 Label the second column 'refined and processed' and the third 'high in fat, salt or sugar'. (If you need a refresher on these concepts, re-read How Processed Foods Cause Overeating on pages 43–7, and Addictive Combinations on pages 49–51.)

4 Now, go through the foods you have listed and mark with a cross the ones that fall into those categories. You may be surprised to find that many of the foods that cause you to overeat fall into one or both of those categories.

My Problem Foods		
FOOD	REFINED/ PROCESSED	HIGH IN FATS, SALT, SUGAR
Ice cream	*	*
Frozen pizza	*	*
Fast-food beefburger	*	*
Shop-bought cake	*	*

As you learn about healthier food choices, refer back to this list and begin consciously to replace these problem foods with healthier options. Use mindfulness to both identify your problem foods and find creative solutions. For example, wean yourself off ice cream by making healthy smoothies with bananas and yogurt. You will still have the sweetness and dairy, but without the refined sugar and high fat that are addictive. If you binge on pizza, try wholegrain pasta with pizza sauce, vegetables and Parmesan cheese. If you love cake, try banana or courgette bread made with wholemeal flour and honey or maple syrup. Instead of cutting out your problem foods completely, which can leave you feeling deprived and miserable, find healthier substitutes for those foods that are satisfying.

EXERCISE 13

IDENTIFYING FIVE PROBLEM SITUATIONS

As with the foods that cause you to overeat, becoming aware of when and where you overeat will help you to develop strategies to cope. You may find this exercise difficult because you believe you overeat all the time. However, if you take some time and really focus, you will probably be able to come up with at least five problem situations.

1 Open your journal at a blank page. On this page list all of the situations that you know cause you to overeat with any details that come to mind. These situations may be a situation or event such as a party or a holiday, or they may be something internal such as an emotional reaction or stress. Your list may look something like this:

• When I'm at a party I tend to eat too many crisps and dip, or cheese and crackers. I feel I can't stop eating and am sometimes embarrassed to look down and find that I have eaten most of the dip myself, or half the cheese plate.
• When I'm at work I tend to snack all day on foods other people bring in. It is hard to resist cakes and sweets.
• When I'm worried or afraid I overeat.
• When I go to my mother's for dinner, I overeat.
• When I'm alone and feeling lonely I tend to watch TV and binge on sweets.

2 Become mindful of your patterns and think of healthier responses that might work for you. Write about these solutions in your journal. For example, you may decide to have a steaming cup of tea with milk when worry strikes instead of the chocolate bar you usually reach for.

Practise mindfulness to become conscious and aware of when you are about to be in a situation where you habitually overeat – such as when you know you are going to be spending the weekend on your own. Then, consciously create a substitute for the high-fat, salty and sugary foods you usually turn to. On the way home from work, drop by the supermarket and, instead of buying your usual crisps and a dip loaded with fat, salt and sugar, buy fresh vegetables and hummus. If eating at a relative's home is problematic for you, use mindfulness to be aware of any tendency to overeat and visualise yourself taking smaller portions and politely refusing seconds and thirds. Mindfulness is a tool to help you take control in situations where you have felt powerless.

Mindfulness Diet: Fruits & Vegetables

You learnt about poor food choices in Part II. Now you will learn about healthy nutrition and what foods you should be including in your Mindfulness Diet. These are healthy, delicious, nutritious foods that can replace your problem foods and make eating in difficult situations easier to manage.

> If it came from a plant, eat it; if it was made in a plant, don't.
>
> MICHAEL POLLAN, AUTHOR
> & FOOD ACTIVIST

Most of the food you eat should be plants – fresh and cooked fruits and vegetables, preferably organically grown. If you are not used to eating many fruits and vegetables, you may feel like putting the book down at this point. But eating a diet of mostly fruits and vegetables is the key to transforming your relationship to your body and to food. Vegetables and fruits are cleansing and healing for the body. Unlike refined and processed foods that are full of chemicals, sugar, unhealthy fats and salt, plant foods normalise your blood sugar, and provide huge amounts of the vitamins and minerals that are absent in much of what is called food by the food industry. Eating more plant foods can help to lower your cholesterol and your weight.

In 2009 the *American Journal of Clinical Nutrition* reported on a study of 97 obese women, all of whom were avoiding high-fat foods. Half the women were instructed to increase their consumption of fruits and vegetables. By the end of

The World of Vegetables

If you have never ventured beyond iceberg lettuce and canned peas, you are in for a treat. The world of plant foods is vast and you can most likely find a very good selection of fresh and good frozen varieties at your local supermarket. Here's a list of vegetables to explore:

Artichoke
Asparagus
Aubergine
Avocado
Beans and peas
    Aduki beans
    Beansprouts
    Broad beans
    Butter beans
    Chickpeas
    Green beans
    Lentils
    Mangetout
    Peas
    Red kidney beans
    Snap peas
Broccoli
Brussels sprouts
Cabbage
Carrots
Cauliflower
Celery
Chard
Chinese leaves
Cucumber
Kale
Kohlrabi
Leeks
Lettuce
    Iceberg
    Little Gem
    Loose-leaf
    Romaine (Cos)
Mushrooms

Mustard greens
Okra
Onions
Pepper (red, green, yellow, orange)
Rhubarb
Root vegetables
    Beetroot
    Carrot
    Celeriac
    Parsnip
    Radish and white radish
    Swede
    Turnip
Spinach
Spring greens
Spring onion
Squashes
    Acorn squash
    Butternut squash
    Courgette
    Marrow
    Patty pans
    Pumpkin
    Spaghetti squash
Sweetcorn
Tomato
Tubers
    Jerusalem artichoke
    Jicama
    Sweet potato
    Yam

a year, the women who were focused on adding vegetables lost an average of 7.7 kg (1 st 3 lb), 20 per cent more than the women who were just paying attention to fat consumption. Shifting your attention to eating healthy foods may therefore be a better way of losing weight than avoiding unhealthy ones.

> To reduce our impact on the environment, we should depend on foods that require little or no processing, packaging or transportation, and those that efficiently convert the energy required to raise them into nutritional calories to sustain human beings. And as you might have guessed, that means we should be increasing our reliance on whole foods, mostly plants.
>
> MARK BITTMAN, COOKBOOK AUTHOR

Vegetables can be stir-fried, steamed, roasted or eaten raw in a salad. Dress them with a little extra-virgin olive oil, lemon juice or fresh herbs. Put them on a skewer, baste them with lemon and olive oil, and then put them under the grill.

It is a good idea to invest in a good vegetable cookbook, or to borrow one from your local library, for preparation and recipe ideas. Start slowly, and simply explore one or two new vegetables a week. Try fresh asparagus in the spring, and

winter squash in the autumn. Record the recipes you tried in your journal, and which vegetables you liked and didn't like. Also, note how you felt – physically, emotionally and mentally – after eating a meal that is composed mostly of vegetables. You can pretty much eat as much as you like of vegetables without this having any effect on your weight. The exception to this might be white potatoes, which are starchy and can cause a blood-sugar imbalance when eaten in excess.

Fruits are full of flavour. However, unlike vegetables, they shouldn't be eaten in huge quantities. You should limit yourself to a couple of pieces or servings of fruit a day, preferably in whole form rather than juiced. Fruit is packed with nutrition but too much fruit can cause your blood-sugar level to increase.

The Mindfulness Diet emphasises pleasure in eating. When you experiment with eating a variety of fruits, be sure to savour the entire experience – shopping for them, washing them, preparing them and sitting down to enjoy them. Record your impressions in your journal. Eat slowly and mindfully and you will learn how rich and satisfying and full of flavour fresh raspberries or ripe melon or a perfect crisp apple can be. Pay attention to how you feel when eating healthy fruits, and how eating two servings daily, over time, affects your sense of well-being and energy.

The Mindfulness Diet emphasises pleasure in eating.

Fruits are in season at different times of the year. Notice when apples are at their best, or strawberries or melons. Talk to the produce person at your local fruit and veg shop and ask him or her to tell you what is in season at the moment. Eating fruits in season will help you enjoy them at their peak. You will discover there are infinite varieties of fruits to explore. For example, there are dozens of varieties of apples and melons available in any well-stocked supermarket. Try them, and learn which ones you prefer.

The World of Fruits

If you rarely eat fruit, or if you are stuck in an apple-orange-banana routine, take this list with you the next time you go to the supermarket. Buy a fruit you have never eaten and give it a go.

Apple	Grapes	Passion Fruit
Apricot	Guava	Peach
Avocado	Kiwi Fruit	Pear
Banana	Kumquat	Persimmon
Blueberry	Lemon	Pineapple
Blackberry	Lime	Plum
Cherry	Mango	Pomegranate
Date	Melon, Cantaloupe	Raspberry
Elderberry	Melon, Water	Star Fruit
Fig	Olive	Strawberry
Gooseberry	Orange	Tangerine
Grapefruit	Papaya	

Mindfulness Diet: Protein

How much protein do you need? Probably not as much as you think, and definitely not as much meat as you think. The meat industries in the Western world would like you to think of protein and meat as synonymous. However, there is plenty of high-quality protein in plant foods. Vegetarians do very well without eating meat. It is not necessary to be a vegetarian to eat healthily, but as you create your mindfulness diet, consider eating meat or dairy only once a day or, better still, only a few times a week. When you do eat meat, chicken or fish, eat small portions, 85–115 g (3–4 oz) at most. Or follow the lead of many non-Western cultures, and treat meat as a condiment that accompanies and enhances the vegetables and grains that make up the bulk of the meal.

When you eat dairy products, choose lowfat versions and try not to have them every day. Experiment with soya milk, rice milk or nut milk in place of cow's milk, to cut down on the amount of saturated fat you consume.

What can you eat for protein besides meat, fish, chicken and dairy? Eggs were once thought to be unhealthy because they are high in cholesterol. But foods high in saturated fat have a more negative impact on your cholesterol levels than foods that contain cholesterol. The new verdict is in: eggs are a good, healthy source of protein. Consider eating bean and grain dishes a few times a week, or stir-fried vegetables with tofu or the fermented version called tempeh. Nuts, eaten in

smaller amounts because of their high-fat content, are another delicious source of protein. Cereals made of wholegrains provide a protein-rich start to the day; try porridge oats topped with soya milk, fruit and nuts for a great breakfast. Whole-grain bread spread with hummus and sliced avocado makes for a delicious lunch, and wholegrain pasta with vegetables and/or beans cooked in a healthy sauce provides a good source of protein for dinner.

Protein is the second most abundant substance in the body after water. It is made up of a compound of amino acids and it takes 20 kinds of these to make the 'complete' protein the body needs. Your body produces about half and the rest you have to get from the foods you eat on a daily basis (these are what are referred to as 'essential amino acids'). If you overeat protein, it is not stored in the body for another day. Your body simply disposes of the protein it doesn't need.

Meat is a complete protein. Beans and grains have to be combined to make up a complete protein, but you don't have to eat them at the same meal to enjoy their benefits. You can have brown rice for lunch and a bean dish for dinner and your body will combine them to meet your protein needs for that day. Vegetables (such as broccoli) contain protein, as does wholegrain bread and pasta.

Cereals made of wholegrains
provide a protein-rich start to the day.

Eating more plant-based sources of protein will help your body heal from years of overeating meat, chicken and dairy – high-calorie foods that are also high in saturated fats. Your cholesterol will become lower and, because you will be eating less fat and calories, your weight will start to fall naturally. Plant-based proteins are filling, so you will definitely not go hungry.

As we mentioned earlier, eating less meat is good for the planet. Reconnecting to the earth and being mindful of its needs is part of healing your relationship with food. Supporting good sustainable farming practices by buying meat from humanely raised animals and organic vegetables from local farms will help you remain mindful of the fact that the needs of your body and the needs of the earth are interconnected.

You don't need to become a vegetarian, but consider eating less red meat, and more chicken and fish. Fish that is high in omega-3 fatty acids, such as wild salmon, is a good choice.

Mindfulness Diet: Carbohydrates

If we were to target two villains in the obesity epidemic, it would be refined and overly processed carbohydrates, such as white breads, biscuits, cakes, crackers, white noodles and pasta, and all forms of sugar, including most chemical sugar substitutes that are used to sweeten foods.

To review, refined flour is usually wholemeal flour that has been stripped of a lot of its nutrients in the refining process: when you eat breads and other foods made of these flours, the

manufacturers may add vitamins back in along with chemicals to preserve 'freshness'. This means that loaf of bread has a long shelf-life. Eating foods made of sugar and refined flour will cause your insulin levels to increase. Insulin tells the body to store fat. Insulin resistance or 'syndrome X' is a by-product of eating too many refined-flour foods.

Other starchy carbohydrates such as white flour or white potatoes can have a negative effect on insulin levels in the body. The body processes carbohydrates as sugars, and refined carbohydrates enter the bloodstream very quickly, causing your blood sugar levels to rise. Food manufacturers like to put sugar in everything because it is addictive and causes you to come back for more. Some fizzy drinks are loaded with corn syrup, another form of unhealthy sugar. High-sugar intake has been connected to spots, infertility, ovarian cysts and uterine cancer in overweight women. Sugar can also interfere with the body's ability to regulate testosterone and oestrogen levels.

If you do use a sweetener, try maple syrup or raw honey in small amounts. Other milder sweeteners are barley-malt syrup and brown-rice syrup. Try to avoid cane sugar, and avoid corn syrup, which is often found in packaged and processed foods and soft drinks.

So, what makes for a healthy carbohydrate? First, all plant foods, not just starchy plant foods, are sources of carbohydrates. Vegetables such as broccoli, lettuce, kale, cauliflower, peppers or aubergine are your best source of carbohydrates. You can eat as much of them as you want, since they are full of soluble fibre and don't cause any problems with your blood sugar. Fruit is also a healthy carbohydrate and is a good source of fibre, but limit yourself to a couple of servings a day as fruit can cause blood-sugar spikes when eaten in excess. Finally, round out your carbohydrate intake with smaller portions of the healthy starchy carbohydrates covered in this section,

---

Wholegrains

Here's a list of wholegrains to try:

Amaranth	Oats
Barley	Quinoa
Brown rice	Rye
Bulgur (cracked wheat)	Spelt
Couscous	Wheat berries
Millet	Wild rice

Search online, or buy or borrow a grain cookbook, for cooking instructions and interesting recipes.

---

including sweet potatoes and winter squashes, wholegrains such as brown rice, wholemeal or quinoa, and pulses like kidney beans, chickpeas or split peas.

When you eat breads, noodles and pastas, choose those that are made with wholegrains, and without any additives or chemicals. Sprouted wholegrains are even better. Foods that are made with 100 per cent wholegrain flours have retained

the nutrients of the grain as well as some additional fibre. The fibre in vegetables and wholegrain bread and pasta acts to slow the spike in blood sugar that refined carbohydrates cause. Fibre also does wonders for your digestion and elimination processes. Look for products made entirely of wholegrains rather than refined flour products with some added wholegrain flour.

Make it your aim to avoid breads and boxed breakfast cereals that have a high level of sugar. A small amount of honey or other natural sweetener is OK. Cakes and biscuits, even if made with wholegrains, are best left for special occasions rather than eaten every day. Choose brown rice and sweet potatoes instead of white rice and white potatoes. In general, it is best to avoid 'the whites'.

Becoming mindful of which carbohydrates are good for you and which are not is the beginning of bringing your body back to balance. Choosing 'good carbs' will facilitate weight loss and balance your mood. Try eating good carbohydrates for a week, and note in your journal how you feel physically and emotionally at the end of the week. Your mind may become sharper as the brain fog caused by excess sugar and refined carbohydrates lifts.

Mindfulness Diet: Fats

Eating fat is not bad for you: you need fat to live. The problem may be that you are consuming too much fat, and also the wrong fats. Here's a short primer on fats.

• **Saturated fat** Saturated fat contributes to high blood cholesterol and tends to raise both good (HDL) and bad (LDL) cholesterol levels. Saturated fat is found mostly in foods from animals, which also contain dietary cholesterol. Coconut oil and palm oil also contain saturated fats. The saturated fat in coconut oil is mitigated by the presence of other nutrients that are good for you, such as lauric acid.

• **Trans fatty acids and hydrogenated fat** During food processing, fats may undergo a chemical process called hydrogenation. Hydrogenated fats are found in margarine, vegetable fats and some cooking oils. Trans fatty acids (TFA) are also formed during the process of hydrogenation. TFA and hydrogenated fats tend to raise the bad LDL cholesterol and lower HDL (the good cholesterols). Some scientists believe TFA raise cholesterol levels more than saturated fats.

• **Polyunsaturated and monounsaturated fats** Polyunsaturated and monounsaturated fats are the two unsaturated fats. They're found mainly in fish, nuts, seeds and oils from plants. Some examples of the food where they are found include salmon, trout, herring, avocados, olives, walnuts and liquid vegetable oils such as soya bean, corn, safflower, rapeseed, olive and sunflower. Both polyunsaturated and monounsaturated fats may help lower your blood cholesterol when used in place of saturated fats and trans fats.

To improve your heart health and lower your cholesterol, you will want to get most of your fats from polyunsaturated and monounsaturated sources. Extra-virgin olive oil is your best choice for everyday cooking and salad dressings. Try to reduce your saturated fat and, if possible, avoid entirely trans fats (TFA) and any food that lists hydrogenated- anything as an ingredient. Instead of butter on your wholegrain bread, try a good-quality, fruity olive oil.

Next, pay attention to how much fat you are eating, and then try to cut down. If you are slathering your bread with butter, and mounding your jacket potato with soured cream and cheese, begin to cut back; you will find you don't really need as much fat as you think for food to taste good. Then try to cut back on the saturated fats, and introduce healthier fats into your diet such as olive oil or linseed oil.

Cutting Down on Sugar & Salt

Because of a decade-long obsession with low-fat consumption, food manufacturers have managed to fill supermarkets with foods that are fat-free but loaded with sugar. The result is a steady increase in the amount of sugar eaten per person, much of it inadvertently, through processed foods. Restaurants add sugar to sauces, salad dressings and entrées to make them more enticing. On average, British people eat 20 teaspoons of sugar per day, whether it's hidden in ready-prepared and processed foods or simply added to foods and drinks.

As people become accustomed to sugary foods, companies make new products even sweeter. It becomes difficult to cut down on sugar because it is so addictive.

Whilst you may be aware of the sugar you add to your breakfast cereal, or coffee or tea, or the sugary jam you spread on your toast, you may not be aware of the hidden sugar found in many products. Unfortunately, sugar can be found in most ready-prepared items, from pasta sauces to salad dressings, breakfast cereals and baked beans. Sugar should be a small part of a healthy diet, and not eaten in the large amounts consumed today, so this is a major reason to stop eating processed foods.

Children in particular are developing taste preferences that can last their lifetime. They can learn a preference for the natural taste of unprocessed, unsweetened foods whilst still young. This will help them live a longer and healthier life.

Here are some strategies for cutting down on sugar:

• Don't go cold turkey: small amounts of sugar added to healthy whole foods are OK, such as a bit of honey on porridge or a teaspoon of maple syrup on winter squash.
• Become a careful label reader: the sugar listed on the nutrition label is a combination of naturally occurring sugar and added sugar. If you spot words ending in '-ose', these are different names for sugar: examples are sucrose, glucose and fructose. Other common sugars found in ingredients are honey, brown sugar, fruit-juice concentrate and corn syrup.

- Don't make puddings a part of every meal: save them for special occasions or have them only once a week.
- Reduce the sugar called for in baking: sugar can often be reduced by up to one-third without affecting palatability.
- Choose healthy alternatives to sugary breakfast pastries: bagels or wholegrain muffins can take the place of doughnuts or Danish pastries.
- Top your cereal with fresh fruit: fresh fruit adds natural and healthy sweetness.
- Use fresh fruit to sweeten natural yoghurt: buy natural yoghurt instead of sweetened yoghurt and mix in fresh strawberries, blueberries, raspberries or banana.
- Make your own frozen treats: buy plastic moulds, or use ice cube trays and freeze 100 per cent pure fruit juices.
- Create energy-boosting smoothies: combine natural yoghurt with banana and fresh fruits in a blender for a delicious home-made smoothie.
- Make your own soft drinks: combine soda water and your choice of fresh fruit juice.

Cutting down on sugar will help you lose weight and avoid diabetes. It is as simple as that. It can help save your life. Becoming mindful of the amount of sugar you are eating – and making sure it is a small amount – is one of the best things you can do for your body and your health. Sodium causes the body to retain fluid. Too much salt makes the heart work too hard

pumping the excess fluid. This can cause hypertension (or high blood pressure), which can lead to heart disease and stroke. In a recent study conducted by the American Heart Association and the University of California, San Francisco, researchers using a computer model discovered that cutting daily salt intake by just under half a teaspoonful (3 g) a day – 30 per cent of the current average intake – could prevent 32,000 strokes and 54,000 myocardial infarctions a year in the USA alone.

Researchers Dr Kirsten Bibbins-Domingo and Dr Lee Goldman suggest that even one-fifth of a teaspoonful (1 g) per day reduction in salt over the next decade would be a more cost-effective strategy for treating hypertension than the cheapest anti-hypertensive drugs. However, Goldman believes we cannot just think of sodium reduction in terms of mea-surements in grams because so much sodium comes from processed and restaurant food. He feels that cutting down salt intake will require food-industry as well as personal efforts.

This is not the first time that excess salt intake has been targeted as a health issue. In November 2009 a study pub-lished in the *British Medical Journal* suggested that cutting salt intake in half – a reduction of roughly a teaspoonful, or about 5 grams a day or – would lower the stroke rate by around 23 per cent and reduce overall cardiovascular disease by as much as 17 per cent. Americans, like people in the UK and many Western countries, take in an average of around two tea-spoonfuls (10 g) of salt a day; the World Health Organization

recommends consuming only one teaspoonful (5 g) per day. Try the following strategies for cutting down on salt without losing flavour in your food:

• Stop cooking with salt. Try replacing salt with pepper, garlic powder, onion powder, basil, oregano, celery seed, sage or dill. Lemon juice, apple cider vinegar or balsamic vinegar will add an alternative zing to vegetables. Halve the salt in recipes for baked goods.

• Remove salt from the table. Replace it with a seasoning of your own such as a combination of garlic powder, onion powder and lemon pepper.

• Read labels carefully when shopping at the supermarket. Compare brands and choose the one with the lowest sodium content. Whenever possible, choose sodium-free varieties, especially in canned goods. If you have regular canned goods you don't want to throw out, rinse the vegetables or fruit in water to remove as much excess salt as possible.

• Limit, or better still, eliminate the saltiest foods from your diet. These include canned meats and fish, ham, sausage, bacon, salted nuts, peanut butter, potato crisps and cheese.

• Avoid ready-prepared meals and processed products. Instead, buy foods that are as fresh as possible and make your meals from scratch – salt-free.

• Avoid salty condiments such as soya sauce, brown sauce, tamari and Worcestershire sauce.

- Make your own salad dressing. Try a combo of extra-virgin olive oil, cider vinegar, garlic and pepper.
- Stay away from fast food. It is loaded with salt as well as sugars and fats.

Becoming mindful of your sodium intake is an important aspect of the Mindfulness Diet. Cut down on salt for a week and then record how this affected your body; do this when you are not experimenting with eliminating other foods. Hopefully, you will have less puffiness and generally feel better. If you use less salt, you will find that over time your taste for it will lessen naturally. Salty foods you enjoyed before cutting down will begin to taste too salty. And that's a good thing.

Food Sensitivities

If you eat a bowl of ice cream, a piece of cheese, or a piece of bread and feel hungrier than before, or if you have cravings for a particular food, you may have what is called a 'food sensitivity'. Food sensitivities may cause people to crave those foods to which they are sensitive, just as a drug addict suffers withdrawal symptoms when the drug is withdrawn. A full-blown food allergy can be life-threatening, causing an immediate violent reaction such as the swelling of the throat. On the other hand, reactions from food sensitivities seem to be delayed from 4 to 48 hours after eating the offending food. For example, you may feel fatigue after eating wheat.

Many overweight or obese people crave and continue to eat those foods to which they are addicted as a way to stop the withdrawal symptoms caused by food sensitivity addiction. The phenomenon is now well accepted by doctors who specialise in the treatment of food allergies and sensitivities. Water retention, or oedema, is particularly common among individuals with food sensitivities and is an important contributing factor to obesity. Removing an offending food will often result in a rapid water loss of 2.25–4.5 kg (5–10 lb) within a week's time.

Dr Michael Rosenbaum, who practises preventive medicine in Mill Valley, California, has observed this water-retention phenomenon frequently among patients in his allergy clinic. He has found that, besides water, food sensitivities can cause the body to retain fat. Dr Rosenbaum believes that food sensitivity most strongly affects the limbic portion of the brain – the portion that controls emotions, memory and functions such as body temperature, sexuality, blood pressure, sleep, hunger and thirst.

The primary food allergens are coffee, dairy products, wheat, eggs, maize and possibly sugar and white potatoes. If you are sensitive to any of these foods, it may be extremely difficult for you to lose weight unless you eliminate the offending food or foods from your diet. Try to eliminate suspect foods from your diet and see if you feel better and/or lose weight.

Elimination Diets

An elimination diet is one way to practise mindfulness of the body. Letting go of a food that you feel you may be causing you problems is a way to practise self-love. At first it will be difficult. For example, if you drop wheat and gluten, you will have to give up noodles, bread, crackers, biscuits and cakes, and you will have to read food labels carefully to make sure you are not eating wheat or gluten in other forms. Gluten is the allergenic part of wheat also found in rye, spelt, barley and oats. If you eliminate dairy from your diet, that includes all dairy products such as milk, cheese, yoghurt, cream, ice cream and butter. Again, it is important to check the ingredients of ready-prepared foods to see if dairy is included.

Choose a food to eliminate from your diet. For 21 days, use your journal to record how you feel, emotionally, physically and mentally after giving up the food you feel may be causing you problems. What can you expect on an elimination diet?

• Expect to understand and appreciate your body better.

• Expect slow results, and allow your body to talk to you. This will take time. Trust your body to tell you what is going on, and trust your journal to help you understand what it is happening.

• Expect to start feeling better if you do have sensitivity to the food you have eliminated. Your energy levels should go up as your symptoms subside.

After 21 days reintroduce the food. Expect your reactions to the offending food to be more noticeable than before. If you are sensitive to that food, years of eating it has put long-term stress on your body. Removing it from your diet gives your body a welcome break and a chance to recover and heal itself. Reintroducing it will give you a strong signal that your body doesn't want it any more.

Experimenting with Smaller Portions

Over the past few decades, portion sizes of everything from muffins to sandwiches have grown considerably. Large quantities of cheap, unhealthy foods have distorted our perceptions of what a typical meal is supposed to look like. According to the American National Heart, Lung and Blood Institute, 20 years ago a serving of pizza was 500 calories, today it's larger and averages 850 calories. Just those extra 350 calories, if consumed twice a month, would add almost 1 kg (2 lb) to your weight in a year or 18 kg (40 lb) in the next two decades. Twenty years ago, a cup of coffee with sugar and cream provided 45 calories, today's fancy coffee drinks can be 330 calories or more. Cinema popcorn tubs also have ballooned in size: once, a tub of popcorn was 270 calories, now it is around 630 calories. A 1996 Cornell University study found that participants who were given larger containers ate more popcorn. Even the venerable bagel has grown from 7.5 cm (3 in) to 12–15 cm (5–6 in) over the last decades. Because portions have become so large, it's hard to understand what a 'serving size' is supposed to be. Additional studies have discovered that larger sizes at restaurants have also contributed to larger sizes at home. According to a 2007 paper published in the *Journal of Public Health Policy*, when McDonald's opened in 1955, its only beefburger weighed around 45 g (1.6 oz); now, the largest beefburger patty weighs 225 g (8 oz). When presented with these larger portion sizes, we have a hard time regulating our intake or working out how much we should be eating. Increased portion sizes give you more calories, encourage you to eat more and distort your perceptions of appropriate food quantities. So, how do you return to eating an appropriate amount of food?

Using the serving size chart on page 58–9, begin now to apply mindfulness to the portion sizes of what you eat. For one week, record in your journal the portion sizes of everything you eat. Try to keep your portions to those listed on the chart. This may seem tedious, but moving from unconscious eating to mindful eating is going to take effort. You will be rewarded with a new conscious awareness, and visual reference, of what a healthy portion size looks like. For example, your jacket potato should be easy to hold in the palm of your hand, and your portion of rice should be the size of a light bulb, not two. If you are in a restaurant that serves giant portions, you will know how much you should eat and what to leave, what is a normal portion and what is not. You can also take home the leftovers for another meal.

Becoming Mindful of Hunger & Fullness

Hara Hachi Bu is a Japanese phrase meaning 'eating until 80 per cent full'. Okinawan islanders practise this way of eating and are known to be one of the longest-living people on the planet. Their longevity is attributed to their moderate calorie intake and to eating plenty of fruits and vegetables, which protects them against free radicals that damage the body's cells.

The Okinawan way of eating is something to, aspire to but what if you don't know when you are hungry or when you are full? To explore your feelings of hunger, begin to estimate how hungry you are several times throughout the day, rather than just at meals. With this exercise, you will become aware of your level of hunger, and you will begin to distinguish between emotional hunger and physical hunger. Through the practice of mindfulness, you can learn to be aware of your hunger without immediately acting on it.

In a world where it is normal to eat at any time, and hunger can be instantly satisfied with fast food, junk food, sweets and other snacks, it is easy to eat as a reflex. Even if the feeling of hunger is very slight, it can cause you to eat. Emotional hunger can manifest as physical hunger. If you suspect you are hungry because you are emotionally upset about something, take a moment to explore what is at the root of your desire to eat. A few minutes of mindfulness practice that focuses on your emotions may calm your hunger pangs and prevent mindless eating. Then again, it may be three or four hours since you last ate, and your body may well be asking for food and nourishment. Over time, you will learn to understand why you are hungry and choose, mindfully, whether to eat or not.

If you have a tendency to be dehydrated, you may find yourself wanting to eat when, really, you are simply thirsty. When you feel hunger outside of meal times, have a glass of water and see if that is what your body needs instead.

When it comes to working with sensations of hunger and fullness, of the two you may find it more challenging to know when you are full. This might take some time to figure out, especially since you may have been ignoring the sensation for years. For one week, simply stop eating when you think you are full. You will be surprised at how little you have eaten, and how much food remains on your plate. You may have been taught to eat everything on your plate when you were a child, and that old message may cause you to overeat after your stomach is full. Know that it is OK to leave food on your plate.

In our fast-paced world it is easy to gulp down food and fail to notice any sensations of fullness. To help you know when you are full, eat very slowly, savour each bite and notice the flavours, which may be simple or more complex. If you eat slowly, you give yourself a better chance of noticing the signs that your body and brain are giving you. After you have worked on knowing when you are full, and you've had some success, take your cue from the long-lived Okinawans, and try to stop eating when you feel 80 per cent full.

MINDFUL FOOD SHOPPING

◆

What you buy matters more than where you shop. If you shop in a supermarket, focus on buying most of your food around the perimeter of the shop where fresh food is located. Try to limit foods from the centre aisles, where most of the packeted and processed foods are shelved. Farmers' markets are another choice for fresh fruits and vegetables. If you have one near you, seek out the sellers with the best-quality produce, and visit them often.

To calm your food cravings and improve your nutrition, buy lots of fresh produce and supplement with some frozen and dried. Frozen peas, corn, broccoli and beans are handy to have available, and dried apricots, dates and bananas make healthy sweet treats. In addition to more perishable produce, stock up on carrots, potatoes and other root vegetables, winter squash and apples. If you do venture into the centre aisles, pick organic canned tomatoes and canned beans, and hearty wholegrain breads and pastas. Buy organic grains and dried beans in small quantities so they stay fresh.

Buy less meat, fish, poultry and dairy, and when you do buy, select the highest quality you can afford. Choose organic eggs and dairy products, and meat from pasture-raised, grass-fed animals reared without hormones and antibiotics. Purchase your animal products from a place you trust. If you are eating fewer animal products, the extra cost of high-quality versions will not break your budget. When it comes to fish, choose varieties that are wild-caught and not endangered. Farm-raised fish may be exposed to contaminates. Some fish have high levels of mercury, and others are safe but overfished. If the label has the Marine Steweardship Council's logo, it has been certified as sustainable seafood. Check online for lists of healthy fish that are not endangered; the Marine Conservation Society's website www.fishonline.org is one source.

If you are hungry when you go food shopping, you will be tempted to buy more food than you need and to buy foods that are high in fat, salt and sugar. To avoid impulse buying, do your food shopping after you have eaten a snack or a meal.

Make a list of what you plan to buy and try to stick to it. There is nothing more frustrating than finding that the fresh vegetables you purchased have gone bad because you forgot you had them, or had no clear plan to use them. If you take a little time to plan your meals for the days ahead, and make a list of the foods and ingredients you will need, it will help you to avoid overbuying, which can lead to waste.

Reading Labels

Despite the Mindfulness Diet emphasis on fresh foods, some foods that are good for you do come packaged. Organic wholegrain pasta and brown rice are good examples. If you buy packaged or canned foods, you can make healthier choices by learning how to read the food label.

In the UK, the ingredients are listed in order of weight, so the main ingredients in packaged food always come first. If the first few ingredients are high-fat ingredients such as cream, butter or oil, then you can be sure the food in question is a high-fat food. One rule of thumb to follow if you want to buy healthy foods is to avoid anything with more than five, familiar-sounding ingredients – that is, ingredients that are recognisable foods. Reject anything with chemicals, preservatives, emulsifiers, stabilisers, gelling agents, thickeners, flavour enhancers or other additives in the ingredients' list. This rule will cut out much ready-prepared foods and keep you from buying most junk food. Knowing what to look for and what to reject will help make your food shopping easier.

Most food labels also contain a nutritional analysis panel. This will usually tell you how many calories there are in a single portion and also how many calories are contained in 100 g (3½ oz). If you are trying to lose weight, you will want to be mindful of the calories you are consuming each day. It's especially useful, then, to know how many calories are contained in one portion of the food you're looking at. But be aware: the manufacturer's concept of a portion is most likely much smaller than yours.

The nutritional analysis panel will also tell you the amount of fat, saturated fat, carbohydrates, sugar, fibre and salt per 100 g (3½ oz). The UK Food Standards Agency has issued useful guidelines to help you decide if a food is high in fat or sugar.

- Low fat = less than 3 g ($^1/_{10}$ oz) of fat per 100 g (3½ oz).
- High fat = more than 20 g (¾ oz) of fat per 100 g (3½ oz).
- Low sugar = less than 5 g ($^1/_6$ oz) of sugar per 100 g (3½ oz).
- High sugar = more than 15 g (½ oz) of sugar per 100 g (3½ oz).

The introduction of a colourful labelling system that uses traffic light colours on the front of many ready-prepared foods makes it easier to monitor the fat, sugar and salt content. This gives an at-a-glance guide to the five key factors:

- Fat content
- Saturated fat content
- Sugar content
- Salt content
- Calories

Red means high, amber means medium and green means low. The more green lights, the healthier the choice. If you buy a ready-prepared food that has all or mostly green lights, you know right away that it's a healthier choice. An amber light means neither high nor low, whilst a red light means the food is high in fat, salt or sugar; these are the foods you should be cutting down on. Try to eat 'red' foods only on occasion. If you want more detailed nutritional information, consult the nutritional panel on the back of the packet, bottle or can.

If you are just beginning to pay attention to food labels, start with the label on a chocolate bar. Did you know that most chocolate bars, besides being high in fat and sugar, contain between 250 and 450 calories? An apple, on the other hand, is sweet, filling and typically contains just 50 calories.

Buying Organic

Most farming relies heavily on artificial chemical fertilisers and pesticides, and there is concern amongst environmentalists and health researchers about the long-term effect of these both on people and on the earth. At the present moment, around 350 different pesticides are permitted. There are government rules in the UK and the USA about acceptable levels of pesticides in food, but it is difficult to believe that ingesting pesticides can be a good thing.

If possible and your budget permits, choose to buy and eat organically grown foods. When a food is sold as organic, it has usually been monitored and certified by one of several organic organisations. Artificial chemical fertilisers and pesticides are strictly limited and antibiotics for animals are kept to an absolute minimum. Animals must have more space and they must be raised to higher welfare standards than those applied to conventionally reared animals.

Organic farming is kinder to wildlife. Without herbicides and pesticides, birds, animals and fish can flourish, and there is no chemical run-off to pollute rivers and streams. Agrochemicals and artificial fertilisers are made from fossil fuels, and therefore organic farming has a lower carbon footprint than conventional agriculture, typically using 27 per cent less energy.

Organic is usually more expensive than conventionally produced food. This is because, typically, crops grown organically are more vulnerable to pests and disease, they are more labour-intensive to grow, and organic animal feed is more expensive. Unfortunately, government subsidies have focused on mainstream farming, keeping the price of conventional foods low in comparison. Buying locally produced organic food directly at a farmers' market is a 'greener' way to shop and can often be less expensive than your supermarket. Conventional food may seem less expensive, but environmentalists have long argued that there are hidden costs in conventional, chemical-dependent farming. For example, it is estimated that consumers in the UK pay about £120 million a year through taxes and higher water bills to clean up pollution. This figure might be reduced if we were prepared to pay slightly higher prices for organically grown food at the till.

Buying Local

It is estimated that there are over 500 farmers' markets in the UK and tens of thousands in the USA, and the number grows each year. A farmers' market allows farmers, growers or producers from a defined local area to sell their own produce direct to the public. All products sold have been grown, reared,

caught, brewed, pickled, baked or smoked by the stallholder. Buying food that is fresh and free of sterile clingfilm can help you in your journey to heal your relationship with food.

> At the farmers' market, freshness is judged by hours, not days.
>
> ALICE WATERS, RESTAURANT OWNER, COOKBOOK AUTHOR

If you buy seasonal produce, grown by local farmers, you will be doing your part to protect the environment. As a bonus, you will find an array of seasonal vegetables not available at your local supermarket such as heirloom tomatoes, or baby beetroots and aubergine, or specialty lettuces and leaves.

When you buy at a farmers' market, you also have the opportunity to slow down and appreciate the effort and love that is put into growing your food. The market makes the impersonal, routine chore of food shopping into something very personal and special. You have the opportunity to meet the farmers who, through their labour, are making it possible for you to eat. You learn to take more care in the choice of your food. Plus, there is something very sensuous and wonderful about buying a juicy, freshly picked, fully ripe tomato or peach. Even organic foods can be cheaper at a farmers' market as there is no middleman involved. Shipping foods across the world contributes to global warming, so buying locally is one way to have a personal impact on climate change and support your local economy.

Switching to Fresh Foods

If you are used to buying food that comes in a box, adding water to it and popping it in the microwave, cooking with fresh foods can seem a little daunting. Fresh foods and vegetables do take more time to prepare, but there are ways to increase your efficiency. Here are some shortcuts that can make your life easier whilst you explore the joys of healthy eating:

• Create a weekly meal plan that uses fruits and vegetables in various ways. For example, enjoy raw apples as a snack, and baked, then topped with natural yogurt for dessert.

• Cook enough to make several meals, and freeze the extra for another day when you are short on time.

• Cook brown rice or beans in larger amounts, save enough for the next day and freeze the rest for use in soups or other dishes. Don't let rice sit at room temperature for long. Either eat it or refrigerate it.

• Try using a slow cooker to make stews and soups.

• Make a big salad for lunch with leftover chicken or fish.

• Make slaws out of thinly sliced or shredded fresh vegetables.

• Keep your kitchen organised, and clean up as you go when preparing food.

• Use a pressure cooker to speed up the cooking of dried beans and wholegrains.

THE JOY OF EATING MINDFULLY

The Mindfulness Diet forgoes discipline and denial, and embraces the sensuous pleasure of healthy eating. It is designed to train your taste buds away from those foods that are addictive and unhealthy, and towards healthy foods that are brimming with taste and nutrition. It is designed to help you recognise the unhealthy practices of the food industry and develop strategies for counteracting them. Through the practice of mindfulness of your body, thoughts and feelings, and knowledge of good nutrition, you can gain control of your eating and your weight. One of the most important ways to heal your relationship with food is to embrace the simple, sensuous pleasure of eating well.

IN A FAST-PACED WORLD, meals tend to be eaten on the run, in front of the TV or standing at the sink. Family members on different eating schedules find it hard to have a meal together. You may view a leisurely meal as a luxury you simply can't afford. If shame over your weight and eating is something that you have absorbed into your psyche, you may wolf down the addictive foods that keep you overweight and unhappy as fast as you can. A meal becomes a 'fix' for your addictions rather than a loving activity in which you eat for enjoyment, to nurture your body and to renew your energy.

EXERCISE 14

A Sensuous Meal

So why not try a different approach, one that makes a meal a sensuous experience? Try this exercise over a weekend when you will have more time and can be on your own.

1 Making use of the previous information about healthy foods, plan a meal for yourself that is balanced and appealing. Go to the supermarket or local farmers' market and buy the ingredients you will need. For example, you might choose a small portion of chicken or fish for your protein, one or two vegetables you enjoy, a fresh salad and a small serving of rice or potato. Your pudding may be a piece of fresh fruit. Take your time buying your food. Notice the beauty, colour and fresh, earthy smells of the produce on display, and pick the most beautiful vegetables and fruits you can find.

2 Decide how you are going to cook what you have bought, and begin your food preparation. Take your time to prepare the meal and notice how it feels to slow down and enjoy cooking.

3 When your meal is ready, serve your meal on a porcelain plate, and sit down at your table to enjoy what you have prepared.

4 Take a moment to look at your beautiful meal. Notice the colours and textures of the vegetables. If you are having rice, notice the individual grains. If you've added herbs, enjoy

the green against the light brown of the rice. If you are having a potato, smell its earthiness. Look at your chicken or fish and inhale its delicious aroma.

5 Now begin to eat slowly, and as you do so, savour each bite. Close your eyes and identify all the flavours that dance on your tongue. If you are having broccoli, for example, notice that it has a slight peppery aspect. Take a moment to taste the sea in your fish, or the delicate sweetness of your chicken breast. Then enjoy the tartness of your salad dressing.

This is a mindfulness practice to help you rediscover the sensuous pleasure of eating. Even though you may not be able to eat in such a leisurely fashion all the time, you can still bring your attention to the sensuous quality of your food at every meal by really tasting what is on your plate.

Liking Your Food vs Loving It

When you begin to be more mindful of what you eat, and can really taste your food and savour its flavours, you will naturally become more discriminating in your food choices. You will no longer mindlessly eat mediocre food, simply because it's there. You will no longer eat food you really don't care for at a party. When you eat mindfully you will begin to distinguish between the foods you really love and enjoy, and the foods you find less enjoyable – and you will gradually lose interest in those foods that fail to meet your higher standards. If you practise mindfulness of the body, mind and emotions regularly, and practise mindfulness when you eat, the foods you love will end up being those that are good for your body.

How does this work? The more you eat slowly and mindfully, the more you recognise freshness and quality in food. You become more appreciative of subtle combinations of flavours and ingredients. You learn to distinguish those foods that make you feel good from those that leave you feeling bloated and uncomfortable. Over time, you will find junk food and other unhealthy foods less appealing. You will begin to find the fat-salt-sugar combinations of processed and fast foods that you may once have liked now cloying and excessively flavoured.

One of the best rewards of mindful eating is that it teaches you to appreciate and love well-prepared, fresh, healthy food. And once you shift to eating that way, you won't want to turn back to your old habits of eating.

The Happy Kitchen

The Mindfulness Diet is designed to bring you back to the kitchen and cooking. If your kitchen has been abandoned for some time, or is cluttered with other aspects of your life such as stacks of bills to pay or your child's science project, it's time to reclaim it for what it is meant to be – a happy, inviting, clean, organised, warm place in which to prepare your food.

• Set aside a day when you are not working, and clean your kitchen from top to bottom, including the cupboards, refrigerator and oven.

• Throw out any old spices, out-of-date products and foods that are loaded with chemicals and additives.

• Assess the usability of your kitchen. Are the pots and pans and their lids in the right place? Are your utensils and oven gloves in easy reach of the oven? Are your kitchen work surfaces clutter-free and ready to use for food preparation? Do you have a good supply of storage containers for leftovers? Take the time to rearrange your kitchen so that it works well for you and makes your cooking easier.

• Assess your kitchen decor. Does the paint need freshening or do the windows need new shades or curtains? Could the space do with some plants and a few baskets for fruits or vegetables? Making your kitchen a pleasant, happy place to be in will help to get you into the routine of cooking and out of the habit of eating ready meals or ordering a pizza.

• Do your dishes, glassware or pots and pans need upgrading? If you don't have the money right now, look for sales and replace these items when you can. If your pots and pans have seen better days, save up so that you can buy high-quality products. Choose heavy-based stainless steel or enamelled cast iron. Avoid aluminium cookware and non-stick pots and pans because the chemical coating eventually comes off and ends up in your food. A standard cast-iron pan, when seasoned, will function nicely as a non-stick pan for omelettes.

• Other useful items to make cooking easier are a blender and a food processor. The blender is great for making smoothies or puréed soups, and the food processor can cut down on time spent on food preparation. Consider forgoing the use of a microwave.

• After you have restored your kitchen to a happy state, step back and appreciate your work. You have used mindfulness of your surroundings to do something very nurturing and loving for yourself.

The Good Energy of the Cook

Food has energy, and so does the cook. The energy of the cook permeates the food. The way in which you prepare meals has a profound effect on how you and others experience it. The quality, appearance, taste, balance and presentation of the food, and how you and others feel after eating reflects the state of your energy – physically, mentally, emotionally and spiritually.

For example, if you are resentful and angry whilst cooking, you will impart a feeling of anger into the food itself, which will diminish its wholesomeness. If you are worried about your budget and select cheaper, poorer-quality foods or provide skimpy portions, you may impart a sense of deprivation, causing those you are feeding to feel unsatisfiedand may binge on junk food. If you cook in a rush in a cluttered, chaotic kitchen, you can lend a feeling of anxiety to your meal, hardly a beneficial quality for nourishing yourself or others.

Whether cooking for yourself or others here are a few suggestions for maximising the positive energy in the food you serve at mealtimes:

• Before you begin, make sure the kitchen is tidy and organised. Clean up as you go and put everything that is not in use in its proper place.

• Start with the best-quality food you can find – fresh, whole, organic, unprocessed and bursting with energy.

• Honour the preparation and cooking of food and be pleased with your efforts, even if you are preparing something as simple as a bowl of porridge.

• Create a peaceful environment for preparing your food. Turn off the TV or CD player, and focus completely on what you are doing.

• Do not wear perfumes or scents that would interfere with the smells of cooking – and may affect your sense of taste.

The method of cooking you use also affects the energy of the food. Food that is cooked quickly without salt such as a stir-fry has a lighter feel. To achieve a more harmonious, sweet and calming taste, cook on low heat for a longer period of time. Pressure-cooking makes the energy in food more concentrated, hearty and strengthening. Steaming adds a moist quality to the food, whereas baking is more warming, and enhances sweet flavours.

Setting the Table

Generations ago, families ate around a table together every night. Today many children are growing up never experiencing a family mealtime, much less how to set the table. Adults may know how, but often don't bother. Because of our 24-hours-a-day eating schedule and busy lives, mealtime is becoming dispensable, and with it the art of setting a table properly. Eating together with family and friends is fun, and it provides a way to slow down and listen to each other. Setting the table can be a calming, centring, mindfulness practice, and it's something you can teach your kids.

If you want to add colour to the table, start with a table-cloth, a table runner or place mats – or to keep things simple, you can skip those altogether. But you will need a dinner plate, glass, knife fork, spoon and napkin for each person. Add a simple centrepiece such as a vase of fresh flowers or a bowl of fruit, and seasonings or condiments, and your table is

> Do all your eating at a table. No, a desk is not a table.
> If we eat while we're working, or watching TV or driving,
> we eat mindlessly – and as a result we eat a lot more
> than we would if we were eating at a table, paying
> attention to what we're doing.
>
> MICHAEL POLLAN, AUTHOR & FOOD ACTIVIST

complete. If you want to add more beauty to the table, lower the room lights and add unscented candles. It also adds to the setting if you know how to position plates and silverware.

So, in case you've forgotten, here's how to position plates and silverware. Place the dinner plates 2.5 cm (1 in) from the edge of the table. Place the knife on the right side of the plate, knife handle at the bottom, blade inwards, 2.5 cm (1 in) from the edge of the table. Make sure the knife is next to the plate but not underneath the plate. The tablespoon is placed next to the knife, also 2.5 cm (1 in) from the edge of the table. The fork is placed on the left side of the dinner plate 2.5 cm (1 in) from the edge of the table, also next to the plate rather than underneath it. The napkin is folded in half and placed next to the fork with the crease furthest away from the fork. The glass is placed above the knife approximately 2.5 cm (1 in) away.

If other silverware is needed for salad, soup or pudding, place the spoons next to the spoons and forks next to the forks. Silverware is placed in order of what is to be eaten, beginning furthest away from the dinner plate and working your way towards the dinner plate. For example, a salad fork would be placed next to the dinner fork, and furthest away from the dinner plate.

Setting a beautiful table honours yourself and your family and friends. It makes eating a conscious activity and helps you slow down and eat more mindfully.

Expressing Gratitude for the Food You Eat

Each piece of food you eat is a symbol of the universe. When you pick up a piece of a broccoli or carrot from your plate, focus mindfully on what you are doing. Take a fraction of a second to identify the food on your fork. Think: 'I am eating a carrot', or 'I am eating broccoli'. When you are mindful, you recognise what you are picking up with your fork, what you are doing in this moment. When you put food into your mouth, know what you are putting into your mouth.

> And when you chew, chew only the carrot, not your projects or your ideas.
>
> THICH NHAT HANH, VIETNAMESE ZEN BUDDHIST TEACHER

When you chew it, know what you are chewing. When you are fully present to yourself and what you are doing, you are fully available to enjoy the moment.

Besides practising mindfulness, one of the best ways to heal your relationship with food is to express gratitude for the food you eat. And one of the best ways to understand gratitude

is to remember the interdependence of everything and everyone in the universe. When you see a carrot on your plate, contemplate that it started as a seed that someone planted in the earth. Rain, sun and the nutrients of the soil caused it to grow. Eventually a person harvested that carrot when it was ripe and ready to eat. A driver delivered the carrot to a wholesale market. A food broker made sure it got to your supermarket, and the produce manager and workers there made sure it was displayed attractively. The person at the till helped you buy it. Thanks to the generosity of all these people, and the support of the earth, you were able to buy this carrot, bring it home and prepare it as part of your meal.

As you eat, take a moment to express gratitude for the earth, the sun, the rain and the many people that made it possible for you to be eating this carrot at this time. Take a minute to remember that many people around the world live in poverty, and express gratitude that you have the means to feed yourself well. Then thank yourself that you are caring for your body by buying, preparing and eating this nutritious food.

Sharing Food with Family & Friends

Sharing a leisurely meal is a great way to relax, to connect with others and enjoy eating slowly and mindfully. If you tend to overeat when alone, you may be prone to eating less in front of others. Providing you are comfortable and relaxed with the friends or family you are eating with, eating communally may have the added benefit of helping you control your consumption.

Entertaining friends and family needn't be stressful. Best that you let go of worries about making a good impression and focus on the love and affection you have for the people you are inviting. The meal can be simple and easy to prepare – perhaps a big pot of soup, or a large green salad, with a great loaf of wholegrain bread, some cheese, a bottle of everyday wine and a jug of water. Add some flowers and a few candles, and you have the makings of a wonderfully nurturing and nourishing evening. Try to get together with friends and family at home as often as you can, and enjoy the pleasure of simple, healthy food and good conversation. Taking the time to connect with those you love and who love you is one of the best antidotes to the stress and alienation of modern living.

> Cooking creates a sense of well-being for yourself and the people you love and brings beauty and meaning to everyday life.
>
> ALICE WATERS, RESTAURANT OWNER, COOKBOOK AUTHOR

You don't always have to cook either. Buffet dinner parties are a great way to get together with loved ones by sharing responsibility for the meal. Just supply the main protein dish, and ask everyone to bring a vegetable dish. Another good way to spend an evening is to invite friends and family over and prepare a meal together. Have fun whilst you cook, and be prepared for a lot of laughter!

MINDFUL RESTAURANT MEALS

◆

Eating in a restaurant can present particular challenges. First the portion sizes may be larger than you need and will tempt you to overeat. If you have been working on cutting down your portion sizes at home, and visualising how big portions of different foods should be, you will have a good chance of controlling your eating. Then, when your food arrives at your table, and the portion of mashed potatoes on your plate could serve a family of four, you will be able to eat appropriately and ask to take home the rest.

IF YOU ARE EATING out with a friend, and you know the portions are oversized at the restaurant you've chosen, consider splitting a main dish, order separate side salads and skip the pudding. You will not be tempted to overeat, and you will both be happy when the bill arrives.

If you are not sure from the description in the menu about how a dish is prepared, ask your waiter. For example, it may not be clear if a chicken dish is breaded and fried, grilled or baked. If you are trying to eat less fat or white flour, make sure to ask so as to avoid unexpected surprises.

Don't be afraid to make special requests either. If you are having a salad, ask for your dressing on the side so you can add a modest amount. If you would prefer an extra portion of vegetables rather than potatoes, or if you don't want white bread on the table, let your waiter know. Most restaurants can accommodate these kinds of request. Choosing wisely from the menu is a good way to make your restaurant dining experience healthier.

It is best to avoid fast-food restaurants, and restaurant chains that are notorious for concocting menu items that are loaded with fats, salt and sugar. They may be less expensive compared to other restaurants, but they are not the bargain they seem. They will compromise your health, and the food is mediocre at best. It is better to save up and go to a restaurant where you will be able to slow down and savour the food. If you choose your restaurant well, the food will be delicious, and the environment will be more conducive to a relaxing, mindful meal.

Choosing Restaurants Wisely

So what kind of restaurant works best with the Mindfulness Diet? Vegetarian or vegan restaurants that serve dishes made with fresh fruits and vegetables, and wholegrains are always excellent choices. Vegetarian restaurants may include eggs and dairy in their menu selections, whereas vegan restaurants will not serve any animal products.

Even avid carnivores are finding the growing number of vegetarian/vegan restaurants a welcome change from their usual meat-heavy fare. Many people are 'flexitarian', that is, they are occasional carnivores who try to improve their health and the health of the planet by eating less meat. There are

increasing numbers of vegetarian restaurants that offer a fine-dining experience – so they are no longer just the hippy cafes they were a few years ago. The new, updated vegetarian menus are sophisticated and satisfying.

Another option is to choose a restaurant that serves the food of a traditional culture such as Japanese, Chinese, Thai, Italian, Greek, Mexican, Latin American or Middle Eastern. Why? These cuisines tend to rely more on grains and other plant foods. If you live in a larger urban area, you will have endless choices. Look for ethnic restaurants that are independent (not a chain of Chinese restaurants, for example), have good reviews and are frequented by people from the culture they represent so that you know the food is authentic. When Chinese restaurant owners strive to make their food more palatable to British or American patrons, they add fat, salt and sugar that would not be in the authentic version. For example, General Tso's Chicken, a standard in American Chinese restaurants, is fried chicken served with a sweet sauce. It would be unrecognisable in China. Restaurants that specialise in bean and grain dishes such as Mexican or Latin American are good choices if they are authentic. If they cater to a Western clientele, then they are best avoided, as you will find your entree loaded with melted cheese and soured cream.

Search out restaurants that pride themselves on the gourmet quality of their food and their expertise with vegetables. Dishes served in these restaurants will tend to be light and subtle in their preparation rather than swimming in fat, salt and sugar. Your food will be served in smaller portions, and you will be encouraged to eat slowly and savour its complex flavours. There are many expensive restaurants in this category, but there are also less expensive options that offer well-prepared, gourmet-quality food in casual settings, at reasonable prices. Some 'gastro pubs' in the UK fit this category. Other restaurants pride themselves on serving organic foods and vegetables from local growers. Their menu is determined every morning based on what is fresh and available that day.

The Mindfulness Diet encourages cooking at home rather than eating out in restaurants. If you save up and make eating out a special occasion, you can enjoy better-quality food and a more pleasurable dining experience. The ideal Mindfulness Diet restaurant would have these qualities:

• A plant-focused menu – primarily one that includes grains, pulses and vegetables, with meat, chicken or fish as a condiment rather than a main course.
• Reasonable portions, which do not overload your plate.
• Subtly prepared dishes, light and full of flavour.
• Fresh, organic, locally grown food.
• A pleasing ambiance that offers an unhurried dining experience.

An ideal restaurant would be hard to find, but the above guidelines can help you make better choices.

MINDFUL EATING AT WORK

◆

Eating mindfully at work is particularly difficult because you are not usually in control of your environment or your time during the working day. You may not have access to a kitchen where you can warm up a meal brought from home, or a pleasant place where you can relax and enjoy what you are eating.

THE BIGGEST OBSTACLE to eating mindfully at work is often snack foods – biscuits, cake, muffins, pastries, sweets or high-fat, high-salt crisps – brought to work by well-meaning co-workers. If you are trying to cut down on these addictive foods, then it can be challenging to have them readily available. You may pass by such foods many times a day and find it difficult not to indulge. Then there is the social pressure to eat cakes brought in for special occasions – birthdays, baby showers, promotions and retirements. It may be that there is a celebration of some kind every week.

How to avoid eating addictive foods at work:

• Have a healthy breakfast before you come to work. If you tend to run late, boil some eggs the night before and pair them with wholegrain toast and a glass of juice or fruit.
• Tell your office mates you are trying to improve your diet and when you decline an offer of a biscuit or a muffin, that you are not trying to offend anyone.

• Be prepared for subtle undermining by those around you who feel threatened by someone trying to eat more mindfully. If it happens, perhaps in the form of a joke, try not to take it personally. Be kind, but be consistent in your refusals.

• Bring your own healthy snacks. Having fresh fruits or nuts to hand will help you fend off the desire to eat office snacks when you get hungry before lunch or late in the afternoon.

• If you are attending a meeting where there will be biscuits and cakes on offer, have something healthy just beforehand to help you to resist the temptation. A crisp, fresh apple, a handful of nuts or a wholegrain muffin should help.

• Bring green or herbal tea bags to work to avoid the temptation to buy from the drinks machine or indulge in a sugary coffee when your energy flags in the afternoon.

• Drink water and stay hydrated – not only because it is good for you, but also because it is easy to confuse hunger and thirst. Aim to drink about eight glasses of water a day. Keep a large bottle of spring water on your desk.

The other major problem area when it comes to eating at work is lunch, particularly if this tends to be a time when workmates socialise. Your colleagues may want to eat at a fast-food restaurant. It's quick and easy, and everyone can get back in the allotted time. If you want to go, try to avoid a high-fat, high-salt and high-sugar combo for lunch if possible. Overleaf are some strategies for sticking to a mindful diet at work.

• Bring your own lunch to work. You can make delicious sandwiches on wholegrain bread, or pack a gorgeous salad, or take a flask of homemade soup or pasta to work when the weather is cold. You will have more time to eat mindfully if you don't have to leave the premises.

• If you don't already have one, ask your boss for a refrigerator so that you and your co-workers can keep the salads and sandwiches you bring from home fresh.

• If you feel that you need to eat out with your workmates once in a while, research the neighbourhood nearby for alternatives to fast-food restaurants that can serve food quickly but has healthy options available.

• If you do want to join your workmates at a fast-food restaurant once in a while, seek out the healthier options on the menu, which many fast-food outlets now provide. Choose a salad option, skipping the high-fat creamy salad dressing, and drink a cup of tea or coffee with your meal.

• In summer eat your lunch outside whenever you can. Explore the neighbourhood around your office to find a park or other green space where you can eat leisurely, enjoy nature and relax for a bit before returning to work.

• If you have a job that involves going out for formal business lunches, you will probably be eating in more upmarket restaurants. Take your time, eat slowly and enjoy your food. Your calm, focused, aware demeanour will help create a positive atmosphere for everyone present.

PUTTING IT ALL TOGETHER

You have been provided with a lot of information in this book. You may feel a bit overwhelmed about what you have learnt or excited about it, or perhaps a little of both.

THE MINDFULNESS DIET, as you have discovered by now, is not a time-limited diet. It is a blueprint for cultivating a new relationship with your body and your mind – one that will help you choose healthy and nourishing foods on a daily basis for the rest of your life. It is based on love and compassion for yourself, knowledge of good nutrition, and a dedication to pleasure and the fine art of eating. It is built on the bedrock of the ancient Buddhist practice of mindfulness. Through this practice, you can slowly, at your own pace, wean yourself away from unhealthy, addictive foods, and replace them with healthy, delicious, succulent plant foods, good-quality fats and high-quality meats. You will learn to eat less and exercise more, and feel better than you have in years, perhaps decades.

There is no rush or deadline. Take your time, write in your journal and stay steady on the path. If one day you eat a chocolate bar or a fast-food burger, the sky will not fall. Love yourself for being human – then make yourself the most healthy and delicious dinner you can imagine and savour every bite.

INDEX

Further Reading

Food

Mark Bittman. *Food Matters: A Guide to Conscious Eating*. New York: Simon & Schuster, 2009.

Annemarie Colbin. *Food and Healing*. New York: Ballantine Books, 1986.

David Kessler. *The End of Overeating: Taking Control of the Insatiable American Appetite*. New York: Rodale, Inc. 2009.

Cynthia Lair. *Feeding the Whole Family: Cooking with Whole Foods*. Seattle: Sasquatch, 2008.

Michael Pollan. *Food Rules: An Eater's Manual*. New York: Penguin, 2009.

Participant Media. Food Inc.: *A Participant Guide: How Industrial Food is Making Us Fatter and Poorer – And What You Can Do About It*. New York: PublicAffairs, 2009.

Matthew Schlosser. *Fast Food Nation: The Dark Side of the All-American Meal*. New York: Houghton Mifflin, 2001.

Mindful Eating

Susan Albers. *Eat, Drink and Be Mindful: How to End Your Struggle with Mindless Eating*. Oakland, CA: New Harbinger Publications, Inc., 2008.

Donald Altman. *Meal by Meal: 365 Daily Meditations for Finding Balance Through Mindful Eating*. Novato, CA: New World Library, 2004.

Jan Chozen Bays. *Mindful Eating: A Guide to Rediscovering a Healthy Relationship with Food*. Boston: Shambhala Publications, 2009.

Thich Nhat Hanh and Dr Lillian Cheung. *Savor: Mindful Eating, Mindful Life*. New York: HarperCollins, 2010.

Mindfulness

Thich Nhat Hanh. *Peace is Every Step: The Path of Mindfulness in Everyday Life*. New York: Bantam, 1991.

Bante Henepola Gunaratana. *Mindfulness in Plain English*. Sommerville, MA: Wisdom Publications, 2002.

Jon Kabat-Zinn. *Coming to Our Senses: Healing Ourselves and the World Through Mindfulness*. New York: Hyperion, 2006